First World War
and Army of Occupation
War Diary
France, Belgium and Germany

32 DIVISION
96 Infantry Brigade
Royal Inniskilling Fusiliers 2nd Battalion
and Manchester Regiment 2nd Battalion
1 January 1916 - 31 January 1918

WO95/2397/1

The Naval & Military Press Ltd
www.nmarchive.com
Published in association with The National Archives

Published by

The Naval & Military Press Ltd

Unit 10 Ridgewood Industrial Park,

Uckfield, East Sussex,

TN22 5QE England

Tel: +44 (0) 1825 749494

www.naval-military-press.com

www.nmarchive.com

This diary has been reprinted in facsimile from the original. Any imperfections are inevitably reproduced and the quality may fall short of modern type and cartographic standards.

© **Crown Copyright**
Images reproduced by permission of The National Archives, London, England, 2015.

Contents

Document type	Place/Title	Date From	Date To
Heading	WO95/2397(1)		
Heading	2nd Bn Roy Innis Fus Jan 1916-Jan 1918		
Heading	2nd Battalion Royal Inniskilling Fusiliers January 1916		
Heading	2 R Inniskilling Fus Jan Vol XVIII		
War Diary		01/01/1916	31/01/1916
Heading	2nd Battalion Royal Inniskilling Fusiliers February 1916		
Map			
Miscellaneous	Trench Map. Area Of Martinpuich		
Heading	2 R Innisk Fus Feb Vol XIX		
War Diary		01/02/1916	29/02/1916
Heading	2nd Battalion Royal Inniskilling Fusiliers March 1916		
Heading	2 R Innisk Fus Vol XX		
War Diary		01/03/1916	31/03/1916
Heading	2nd Battalion Royal Inniskilling Fusiliers April 1916		
Heading	2 R Innisk Fus Vol XXI		
War Diary		01/04/1916	30/04/1916
Heading	2nd Battalion Royal Inniskilling Fusiliers May 1916		
War Diary		01/05/1916	31/05/1916
Heading	2nd Battn. The Royal Inniskilling Fusiliers June 1916		
War Diary		01/06/1916	30/06/1916
Heading	War Diary 2nd Battn. The Royal Inniskilling Fusiliers. July 1916		
Miscellaneous			
Heading	War Diary 2nd R. Inniskilling Fusiliers 1st July 1916-31st July 1916 Vol 24		
War Diary		01/07/1916	31/07/1916
Heading	War Diary 2nd Battn. Inniskilling Fusiliers. August 1916		
Miscellaneous	D.A.G., The Base.	06/12/1916	06/12/1916
Heading	War Diary Of 2nd Battalion Royal Inniskilling Fusiliers. From 1st August 1916 To 31st August 1916 Volume XXV		
War Diary		01/08/1916	31/08/1916
Heading	2nd Battn. Inniskilling Fusiliers. September 1916		
Heading	War Diary. Of 2nd Battalion Royal Inniskilling Fusiliers. From 1st September 1916 To 30th September 1916 Volume 25		
War Diary		01/09/1916	30/09/1916
Heading	2nd Battalion. Royal Inniskilling Fusiliers. October 1916		
Heading	War Diary Of 2nd Royal Inniskilling Fusiliers From 1st October 1916 To 31st October 1916 Volume 27		
War Diary		01/10/1916	31/10/1916
Heading	2nd Battalion Inniskilling Fusiliers. November 1916		
Heading	War Diary. 2nd R. Inniskilling Fusiliers. November 1st To 30th 1916 Vol 28		
War Diary		01/11/1916	30/11/1916
Heading	2nd Battalion Royal Inniskilling Fusiliers. December 1916		

Heading	War Diary Of 2nd Royal Inniskilling Fusiliers From 1st December 1916 To 31st December 1916 Volume XXIX		
War Diary		01/12/1916	31/12/1916
Miscellaneous			
War Diary		01/01/1916	31/01/1916
Heading	War Diary Of 2nd Royal Inniskilling Fusiliers From 1st February 1917 To 28th February 1917 Volume XXXI		
War Diary	In The Field	01/02/1917	28/02/1917
Heading	War Diary Of 2nd Bn. Royal Inniskilling Fusiliers. From 1st March 1917 To 31st March 1917 Vol 32		
Heading	War Diary Of 2nd Royal Inniskilling Fusiliers From 1st March 1917 To 31st March 1917 Volume XXXII		
War Diary		01/03/1917	31/03/1917
Miscellaneous			
Heading	War Diary Of 2nd Royal Inniskilling Fusiliers. From 1st April 1917 To 30th April 1917 Vol XXXIII		
Heading	War Diary Of 2nd Royal Inniskilling Fusiliers From 1st April 1917 To 30th April 1917 Volume XXXIII		
War Diary		01/04/1917	31/05/1917
Heading	War Diary Of 2nd Batt Royal Inniskilling Fusiliers From 1st June 1917 To 30th June 1917 Volume XXXV		
War Diary		01/06/1917	30/06/1917
Heading	War Diary Of 2nd Royal Inniskilling Fusiliers. July 1917 Vol 36		
War Diary		01/07/1916	31/07/1916
Heading	War Diary Of 2nd Batt Royal Inniskilling Fusiliers From 1st August 1917 To 31st August 1917 Volume XXXVII		
War Diary		01/08/1917	31/08/1917
War Diary		01/09/1917	30/09/1917
War Diary	La Panne Coxy De	01/10/1917	02/10/1917
War Diary	Bray Dunes	02/10/1917	25/10/1917
War Diary	La Casino	25/10/1917	25/10/1917
War Diary	Eringham	26/10/1917	31/10/1917
War Diary		01/11/1917	30/11/1917
War Diary	Canal Bank	01/12/1917	09/12/1917
War Diary	Wurst Farm (support Battn)	09/12/1917	10/12/1917
War Diary	Front Line	10/12/1917	12/12/1917
War Diary	Wurst Farm	13/12/1917	13/12/1917
War Diary	Dambre Camp	17/12/1917	21/12/1917
War Diary	Hilltop Farm	25/12/1917	26/12/1917
War Diary	Fus Coys Irish Farm	27/12/1917	28/12/1917
War Diary	Hilltop Farm to Bonnigues	29/12/1917	29/12/1917
War Diary	Bonnigues	30/12/1917	19/01/1918
War Diary	Dirty Bucket Camp	21/01/1918	21/01/1918
War Diary	Canal Bank	22/01/1918	23/01/1918
War Diary	Larry Camp	25/01/1918	29/01/1918
War Diary	Front Line	29/01/1918	31/01/1918
War Diary	Hospital Farm	31/01/1918	31/01/1918

WO97/23971(1)
WO95/23970

WO95/23970(1)

32ND DIVISION
96TH ~~BRIGADE~~ Brigade

2ND BN ROY. INNIS. FUS
JAN 1916–JAN 1918

FROM 2 DIV S. BDE

To 36 DIV 109 BDE

96th Brigade.
32nd Division.

Battalion came from G.H.Q. 1.1.16

2nd BATTALION

ROYAL INNISKILLING FUSILIERS

JANUARY 1 9 1 6

18.H.

J R Inuiskilling Fus
Jan
Vol XVIII 26/32

Copied from GHQ, Jan 1st

2nd Royal • Inniskilling Fusiliers.

Army Form C. 2118.

WAR DIARY
INTELLIGENCE SUMMARY.
(Erase heading not required.)

Instructions regarding War Diaries and Intelligence Summaries are contained in F. S. Regs., Part II. and the Staff Manual respectively. Title pages will be prepared in manuscript.

Hour, Date, Place		Summary of Events and Information	Remarks and references to Appendices
1916.			
January	1st.	In billets at LAVIEVILLE and MILLENCOURT.	
"	2nd.	Battn. inspected by Brig. Gen. C. Yatman, comdg 96th Infy. Bde. Strength on parade - 28 Officers 960 other ranks.	
		Orders for move to 36 (Ulster) Division cancelled. Battn. to remain in 96th Infy. Bde. Battn. took over trenches in B. 2. Subsector, AUTHUILLE on night of 2nd, from 1/8 Liverpool Regt. & 2/5 Lancs Fusrs. 16th Lancs Fusrs. on our right, and Hampshire Regt. (4th Div.) on our left.	
"	2 – 6	Battn. remained in trenches in B. 2. Sub. sector, AUTHUILLE. Casualties - O.Ranks - killed one, Nod.W.I.O.	
"	6	Bn. relieved in B. 2. Subsector by 16th Northumberland Fusrs., and marched to billets in Div. Res. at MARTINSART.	
"	6 – 10	In billets at MARTINSART (Div. Reserve). 2 Officers and 100 other ranks provided garrison at MOUND KEEP, relieved on 9th inst. by 4th Div. 1 Officer and 30 other ranks then took over McMAHON'S POST from 4th Div. Battn. found working parties for work on Reserve trenches.	
"	10	Marched to billets in Corps Reserve at SENLIS.	
"	10 – 18	In billets at SENLIS. Furnished working parties of 3 Officers and 250 other ranks daily for work on intermediate line at BOUZINCOURT. Instruction of Grenadiers and Machine Gunners carried on whilst in Reserve. Reinforcements - 39 other ranks joined 14th.	

Army Form C. 2118.

WAR DIARY
~~INTELLIGENCE~~ SUMMARY.
(Erase heading not required.)

Instructions regarding War Diaries and Intelligence Summaries are contained in F.S. Regs., Part II. and the Staff Manual respectively. Title pages will be prepared in manuscript.

Hour, Date, Place		Summary of Events and Information	Remarks and references to Appendices
1916.			
January	17.	Gen. Sir Douglas Haig, Commander-in-chief passed through our lines, and expressed his satisfaction with the smartness of guards, etc.	
"	18.	Battn. took over AUTHUILLE defences from 1st Dorset Regt. Furnished 2 platoons as garrison at GORDON CASTLE. Remainder of Bn. employed at work on trenches, etc. under R.E.	
"	18-21	As above.	
"	21.	Took over F.2. Sub-sector AUTHUILLE from 16th Northumberland Fus'rs. 16th Lancs. Fus'rs on our right, and 11th Div. on our left.	
"	21-26	In trenches in F.2. Sub-sector, AUTHUILLE. Different small enterprises were undertaken during our tour, and artillery was very active on both sides. Casualties – Capt. F.C. Mourtray and Lieut. B.T. Bucknall wounded 22nd inst. 1 other ranks – Died of wounds one; wounded 9. Reinforcements – 40 other ranks joined Bn. 23rd inst.	
"	26	Battn. relieved in F.2. Sub-sector by 15th H.L.I. and marched to billets in Corps Reserve at SENLIS.	
"	26-31	Remained in billets at SENLIS. Battn. furnished permanent "wiring" party of 2 officers and 50 other ranks under Capt. C.C. Thompson, also permanent "digging" party of 2 officers and 150 other ranks, under 2/Lieut. L.A. Woodley. These parties were practically both by day and

Army Form C. 2118.

WAR DIARY
or
INTELLIGENCE SUMMARY.
(Erase heading not required.)

Instructions regarding War Diaries and Intelligence Summaries are contained in F.S. Regs., Part II. and the Staff Manual respectively. Title pages will be prepared in manuscript.

Hour, Date, Place	Summary of Events and Information	Remarks and references to Appendices
1916.		
January 26-31 Continued.	day and night in wiring and "digging" respectively, in view of their being required on an interprise at an early date. Working parties of 6 Officers and 300 other ranks were provided daily for work on new road at BOUZINCOURT. Several alarms of gas attacks were received, but these usually proved false.	
January 31.	About 4.45 p.m. Bn. was ordered to be held in readiness to move to support the 18th Div. which was being attacked by the enemy on our right. About 9 p.m. orders were received that Battn. would not be required, as the attack had proved unsuccessful. During the month Officers and other ranks were detailed to attend short courses at Machine Gun School, Grenade School, 3rd Army School of Instruction, and instruction in Telescopic Sights. A number were granted leave to England.	

31/1/16.

C.R.W. Alexander Capt & A. Lieut. Colonel,
Commanding 2nd Royal Inniskilling Fusiliers.

96th Brigade.
32nd Division.

2nd BATTALION

ROYAL INNISKILLING FUSILIERS

FEBRUARY 1 9 1 6

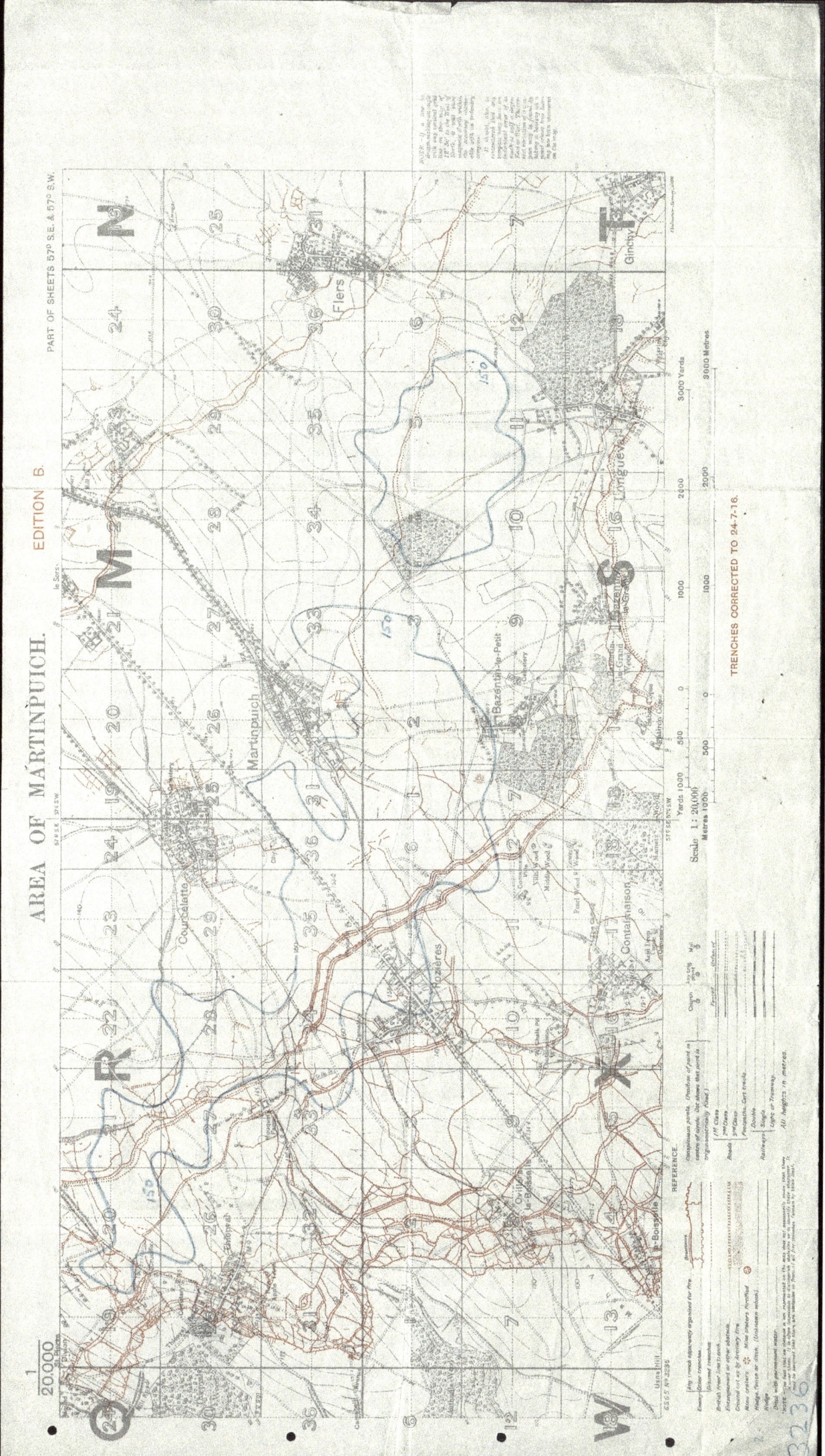

TRENCH MAP.

AREA OF MARTINPUICH.

Scale 1 : 20,000.

EDITION B.

XXX̶X̶ 640/32
(96)

2 R Inniske Fus

Feb

Vol XIX

2nd Royal Inniskilling Fusiliers.

Army Form C. 2118.

WAR DIARY
or
INTELLIGENCE SUMMARY.
(Erase heading not required.)

19. H.

Hour, Date, Place	Summary of Events and Information	Remarks and references to Appendices
1916.		
February 1st to 6th.	Battn. remained in billets in Corps Reserve at SENLIS. Working party of 6 Officers and 300 other ranks were found daily for work on new road at BOUZINCOURT. The "wiring and digging parties" referred to in Diary 26-31 January 1916, took part in a successful enterprise on the night 2/3 Feby. 1916 without casualties. Capt. G.G. Thompson was in charge of the "wiring" parties furnished by 96th Bde. Lieut. Col. G.A. Wilding. C.M.G. was promoted temporary Brigadier Genl. to command 10th Infy. Bde. and proceeded to take over his duties on 4th inst. Major J.H. Crawford D.S.O. assumed command of the Battn. from that date.	
February 6th.	Battn. took over trenches in G.1. Sub-Sector, AUTHUILLE, relieving the 2nd Manchesters with Bde. 16th Lancs. on our left and 2nd K.O.Y.L.I. 97th Bde. on our right.	
February 6th to 13th.	Battn. remained in trenches in G.1. Sub-Sector. Artillery and Trench Mortars were active on both sides during this tour. On the evening of the 9th inst. the enemy opened heavy artillery	

Army Form C. 2118.

WAR DIARY
or
INTELLIGENCE SUMMARY.
(Erase heading not required.)

Instructions regarding War Diaries and Intelligence Summaries are contained in F. S. Regs., Part II. and the Staff Manual respectively. Title pages will be prepared in manuscript.

Hour, Date, Place	Summary of Events and Information	Remarks and references to Appendices
February 6th to 13th (Continued)	Artillery fire chiefly lachrymatory shells against F2. Sub-sector and extreme right of our sector. Little damage was done in our sector and no casualties during this bombardment. Casualties during tour in trenches — Other ranks, killed 8, wounded 17.	
February 13th.	Battn. was relieved by 5th K.O.Y.L.I. and 5th York & Lancs. 148th Bde., 49th Divn. and marched to quarters in huts at HENENCOURT.	
February 13th to 17th.	In huts at HENENCOURT, weather very wet and training impossible.	
February 17th.	Marched to billets in ALBERT, with one company at AVELUY KEEP, relieving the 11th Border Regt. 97th Bde.	
February 17th to 24th.	Remained in billets in ALBERT and AVELUY as above. Battn. furnished working parties of 5 Officers and 300 other ranks daily for work on front line and support trenches in F. sector, etc. Casualties on working parties — Other ranks, killed 1, wounded 1.	
February 24th.	Battn. took over trenches in F2. sub-sector, AVELUY, from the	

Army Form C. 2118.

WAR DIARY
or
INTELLIGENCE SUMMARY.

(Erase heading not required.)

Instructions regarding War Diaries and Intelligence Summaries are contained in F. S. Regs., Part II. and the Staff Manual respectively. Title pages will be prepared in manuscript.

Hour, Date, Place	Summary of Events and Information	Remarks and references to Appendices
February 24th (continued)	The 16th Northumberlands, 16th Lancs, on our right and 5th York & Lancs, 148th Bde, 49th Divn, on our left. "A", "C" and "D" Coys in front line. "B" Coy in reserve. A detachment of 11th Bde. Machine Gun company was allotted to Battn. sector.	
February 24th to 29th.	Remained in trenches in F.2 sector, AVELUY.	
February 29th.	Very heavy shelling of enemy's trenches by our artillery. The enemy retaliated with heavy shells on AUTHUILLE WOOD and Battn. Hd. Qrs. Little damage was done. Two additional Lewis guns were received making a total of 6 with Battalion. Casualties during this tour — other ranks, wounded 3. 2/Lieuts. G. E. Baker, F. Young and R. W. Boyle, 12th Royal Inniskilling Fusiliers joined for duty 16th inst. Reinforcements — other ranks 17, joined 27th inst. During the periods out of trenches, men were trained in grenade throwing and rapid firing. During month, Officers & other ranks attended courses of instruction at 96th Bde. Grenade School, Bn. Lew. School, WISQUES & school of telescopic sights.	[signature] Major Commdg. 2nd Bn. Inniskilling Fus. 2nd. Bn. ROYAL INNISKILLING FUS. No. 173/16 Date

(9 29 6) W 2794 100,000 8/14 H W V Forms/C. 2118/11

96th Brigade.
32nd Division.

2nd BATTALION

ROYAL INNISKILLING FUSILIERS

MARCH 1 9 1 6

CHQ/32

J.R. Inniskl. Fus
Vol XX

20-H

Army Form C. 2118.

WAR DIARY
or
INTELLIGENCE SUMMARY.
(Erase heading not required.)

Instructions regarding War Diaries and Intelligence Summaries are contained in F. S. Regs., Part II. and the Staff Manual respectively. Title pages will be prepared in manuscript.

Hour, Date, Place	Summary of Events and Information	Remarks and references to Appendices
1916		
March 1st.	Remained in trenches in F.2. Subsector, AVELUY.	
March 2nd.	Relieved by 16th Northumberland Fus, and took over billets at AVELUY. "A" Coy in dugouts at CRUCIFIX CORNER.	
March 2nd – 5th.	Remained in billets at AVELUY. The Battalion furnished working parties daily for work in front line and support trenches.	
March 6th.	Relieved 4th West Ridings 49th Division in AUTHUILLE defences. "C" Coy remained at AVELUY.	
March 6th – 7th.	In AUTHUILLE defences. Furnished working parties under R.E. for work on front line trenches daily.	
March 8th.	Took over trenches in F.2. Subsector, AVELUY from 16th Northumberland Fus. 19 Lanc Fus, 14th Bde on our right, 16 Lanc Fus on our left.	
March 9th.	About 11 p.m the enemy bombarded our lines with trench mortar and shells of all calibre. Our artillery retaliated and an intense artillery duel ensued, lasting over one hour.	
March 8th – 11th.	In trenches as above. Casualties – Other ranks – killed 3 wounded 7.	

Army Form C. 2118.

WAR DIARY
or
INTELLIGENCE SUMMARY.
(Erase heading not required.)

Instructions regarding War Diaries and Intelligence Summaries are contained in F.S. Regs., Part II. and the Staff Manual respectively. Title pages will be prepared in manuscript.

Hour, Date, Place	Summary of Events and Information	Remarks and references to Appendices
1916		
March 12th.	Relieved by 15th Lanc Fus and took over billets at BOUZINCOURT. In Bde Reserve. 'D' Coy in dugouts at CRUCIFIX CORNER. Working parties were furnished by Battalion daily for work on front line and support trenches.	
March 12th - 15th.	In billets as above.	
March 16th.	Relieved 16th Northumberland Fusrs in G.1. Subsector, 9th Inniskillings (Ulster Divn) on our left, 16th Lanc Fus on our right.	
March 17th.	St Patrick's Day - Shamrock was issued to Battn. at 'Stand to'. The enemy's artillery and trench mortars were very active throughout the day.	
March 16th - 19th.	In trenches as above. Casualties - Wounded 2/Lt. A.H.H. Armstrong. Other ranks Killed 5, Wounded 38.	
March 20th.	Relieved 16th Northumberland Fusrs in dugouts at AUTHUILLE defences.	
March 20th - 23rd.	In AUTHUILLE defences. Battalion furnished working parties daily for work on front line and support trenches.	

Army Form C. 2118.

WAR DIARY
or
INTELLIGENCE SUMMARY.
(Erase heading not required.)

Instructions regarding War Diaries and Intelligence Summaries are contained in F.S. Regs., Part II. and the Staff Manual respectively. Title pages will be prepared in manuscript.

Hour, Date, Place	Summary of Events and Information	Remarks and references to Appendices
1916	3	
March 24th	Relieved 16th Northumberland Fus. in G.1. Subsector. 10th Inniskillings (Ulster Divn) on our left. 16th Lanc. Fus. on our right.	
March 26th	Heavy shelling of our sector by hostile trench mortars. About 80 "Oilcans" fell, doing much damage to trenches. "A" Coy's Hd. Qrs was completely blown in.	
March 24th - 27th	In trenches as above. Casualties - Other ranks. wounded 7.	
March 28th	Relieved by 15th Lanc. Fus. and took over billets at BOUZINCOURT, in Bde. Reserve. "B" Coy in dugouts at CRUCIFIX CORNER.	
March 28th - 31st.	In billets as above. Battn. furnished working parties, daily, for work on front line and support trenches.	

31/3/16

[signature] Major.
Commdg. 2nd Bn. Royal Inniskilling Fus.

96th Brigade.

32nd Division.

2nd BATTALION

INNISKILLING FUSILIERS

APRIL 1 9 1 6

GHO/32

2 R. Innisk Fus

Vol XXI

Army Form C. 2118.

2nd Battalion, Royal Inniskilling Fusiliers.

WAR DIARY
or
INTELLIGENCE SUMMARY.
(Erase heading not required.)

Instructions regarding War Diaries and Intelligence Summaries are contained in F.S. Regs., Part II. and the Staff Manual respectively. Title pages will be prepared in manuscript.

21.M

Hour, Date, Place	Summary of Events and Information	Remarks and references to Appendices
1916		
April 1st – 3rd	In billets at BOUZINCOURT, in Divisional reserve.	
" – 3rd.	Marched to billets at WARLOY.	
" – 4th	Marched to billets at RUBEMPRE. During stay at RUBEMPRE, Battn. was exercised in company, battalion, brigade and divisional training.	
" – 23rd.	Marched to billets at BOUZINCOURT, in Divisional reserve.	
" – 24th.	Battn. took over trenches in AUTHUILLE sub-sector from 17th H.L.I. in 14th Bde. 2nd West Yorkshire Regt. 23rd Bde, 8th Divn. on our right. 16th Lancs. 96th Bde, 32nd Divn. on our left. Casualties – other ranks, 4 killed, 7 wounded.	
" – 28th	Relieved in AUTHUILLE sub-sector by 16th N.F. and took over defences of AUTHUILLE. Battn. furnished working parties of 8 officers and 500 other ranks daily for work on front line and support trenches.	
" – 28th – 30th	As above.	
	During the month, Officers, N.C.O's & men attended classes of instruction in 3" Stokes Mortars, Lewis and Vickers Guns. Bayonet.	

(9 29 6) W2794 100,000 8/14 HWV Forms/C. 2118/11

WAR DIARY
or
INTELLIGENCE SUMMARY.
(Erase heading not required.)

Army Form C. 2118.

Hour, Date, Place	Summary of Events and Information	Remarks and references to Appendices
	2	
	Bayonet fighting, Bangalore Torpedoes and Bombing. 2/Lieut. L. H. Charles, 2/Lieut. J. R. McIlroy and 2/Lieut. K. L. Paterson, 4th Bn. Rl. Inniskilling Fusrs. joined Bn. for duty 18.4.16. 2/Lieut. G. A. Webb, 4th Rl. Inniskilling Fusrs. joined 23rd April. 2/Lieut. G. Hawksley, 4th Bn. Rl. Inniskilling Fusrs. joined 24th April. Lieut. L. G. Palmer, 15th Rl. Inniskilling Fusrs., 2/Lieuts. J. R. Horwood, F. R. Orpwood, J. J. Huskinson, 4th Rl. Inniskilling Fusrs. joined 25th April. Reinforcements — other ranks — 79 arrived on 10.4.16; 4 on 14.4.16; 8 on 17.4.16 and 7 on 25.4.16.	
1/5/'96.		

T. MacGee Major.
Commanding 2nd Bn. Royal Inniskilling Fusrs.

96th Brigade.
32nd Division.

2nd BATTALION

INNISKILLING FUSILIERS

M A Y 1 9 1 6

2nd Battn. Royal Inniskilling Fusiliers

WAR DIARY
or
INTELLIGENCE SUMMARY.

Army Form C. 2118.

Hour, Date, Place	Summary of Events and Information	Remarks and references to Appendices
1916.		
May 1st.	In AUTHUILLE defences. The battalion furnished a "digging" and "wiring" party of 7 Officers and 240 other ranks for an enterprise which was successfully carried out. Casualties - O.R. killed - one.	
May 2nd.	Relieved 16th N.F. in AUTHUILLE subsector. 16th Lancs on our left. 2/West Yorks, 23rd Bde., 8th Divn. on our right.	
May 2nd — 6th.	In trenches as above. At 12 midnight 5th/6th our artillery opened a heavy bombardment along the whole of our front, in order to cover a raid which was successfully carried out by the 19th Lancs. Our casualties were O.R. killed two, wounded fourteen.	
May 6th.	Relieved in AUTHUILLE subsector by 19th Lancs, 14th Bde., and marched to billets at WARLOY.	
May 6th — 12th.	In billets at WARLOY.	
May 13th.	Battn. took over billets vacated by 16th N.F. at BOUZINCOURT in Divl. reserve.	
May 13th — 16th.	In billets at BOUZINCOURT. Battalion furnished working parties of 8 officers & 400 O.R. daily for work on front line.	

Army Form C. 2118.

WAR DIARY
or
INTELLIGENCE SUMMARY.

(Erase heading not required.)

Instructions regarding War Diaries and Intelligence Summaries are contained in F.S. Regs., Part II. and the Staff Manual respectively. Title pages will be prepared in manuscript.

Hour, Date, Place	Summary of Events and Information	Remarks and references to Appendices
1916.		
May 17th	Line and support trenches	
	Batts marched to RUBEMPRE and took over billets vacated	
	by the 17th H.L.I.	
May 17th – 23rd	In billets at RUBEMPRE. Batt. was exercised in Company,	
	Brigade and Divl. training	
May 24th	Batts. took over huts in CONTAY WOOD	
May 24th – 29th	In huts at CONTAY WOOD	
May 29th	Marched to billets in SENLIS	
May 30th	Batts. relieved 16th H.L.I., 97th Bde. in AUTHUILLE defences	
May 31st	In AUTHUILLE defences. Working parties of 10 officers and	
	600 other ranks found for work on front line & support	
	trenches.	
	During the month 2/Lieuts. A.C.B. Wallacott, L.P. Hawkoot, P.J.	
	O'Ryan, J/Rl. Irnis. Fus. and 2/Lieuts. L. Rayner Smith, A.H. Tottenham and	
	W.P. Sweeney, 7/Rl. Innis. Fus. joined for duty. Other ranks 98.	

J. W. Crawford Lieut. Colonel
Commdg. 3/Royal Inniskilling Fus rs.

(9 29 6) W 2794 100,000 9/14 H W V Forms/C. 2118/11

96th Inf. Bde.
32nd Div.

2nd BATTN.　THE ROYAL INNISKILLING FUSILIERS

JUNE

1916

2nd Royal Inniskilling Fusiliers
96/5 2 R Inniskilling Fus Vol 23

WAR DIARY
INTELLIGENCE SUMMARY.
(Erase heading not required.)

Hour, Date, Place	Summary of Events and Information	Remarks and references to Appendices
1916		
June 1 & 2.	In AUTHUILLE Defences. Working parties of 14 officers and 400 other ranks found daily for work on front line and support trenches.	
3rd.	Battn. relieved 16th Northumberland Fus. in THIEPVAL Sub-Sector. 16th Lancs. on our right, 36th (Ulster) Div. on our left.	
" 3 – 4	In trenches in THIEPVAL Subsector. Casualties – Other ranks killed 4, wounded 24.	
" 4th	Relieved by 16th Northumberland Fus., and took over AUTHUILLE Defences	
" 4 – 13th	In AUTHUILLE Defences. Working parties of 20 officers and 400 other ranks found daily for work on front line and support trenches.	
" 13th	Battn. relieved in AUTHUILLE Defences by 1st Dorset Regt. 1HKS Bde. and took over billets in Div. Reserve in SENLIS.	
" 13 – 22.	Bn. remained in billets in Div. Reserve in SENLIS. Exercised in Coy., Bn., Bde. and Div. Training.	

Army Form C. 2118.

WAR DIARY
INTELLIGENCE SUMMARY
(Erase heading not required.)

Instructions regarding War Diaries and Intelligence Summaries are contained in F.S. Regs., Part II. and the Staff Manual respectively. Title pages will be prepared in manuscript.

Hour, Date, Place	Summary of Events and Information	Remarks and references to Appendices
1916		
June 21st.	Battn. was inspected by the G.O.C. 32nd Div., who expressed himself highly pleased with the good turn out on parade, and thanked all ranks for their good work during the Winter. He also expressed himself confident that the Battn. would cheerfully carry out any undertaking they might be called upon to perform in the near future.	
22nd.	Battn. marched to MARTINSART WOOD and bivouacked.	
23rd.	Bn. took over AUTHUILLE Defences and bivouacked.	
23 – 26th.	In AUTHUILLE Defences. Bombardment of enemy line commenced.	
26th.	Relieved 16th Lanc. Fusrs. in trenches in THIEPVAL Sub-Sect.	
26 – 30th.	In trenches in THIEPVAL subsect. Bombardment continued. Casualties:– Major E.J. Saunders wounded. 2/Lieut. A.H. Tottenham killed. Other ranks:– Killed 3. wounded 29. Patrols were sent out and gained useful information for which the Bn. was complimented by the Div. and Bde. Commander.	

A Blackey Lieut for Lieut. Colonel,
Commanding 2nd Royal Inniskilling Fusrs.

96th Inf.Bde.
32nd Div.

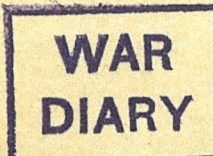

2nd BATTN. THE ROYAL INNISKILLING FUSILIERS.

J U L Y

1 9 1 6

5.

Army Form C. 2118.

WAR DIARY
or
INTELLIGENCE SUMMARY

(Erase heading not required.)

9618.
/32 Div. July

Vol 24

CONFIDENTIAL
WAR DIARY
2nd R. Inniskilling Fusiliers

1st July 1916 — 31st July 1916

ORIGINAL

Place	Date	Hour	Summary of Events and Information	Remarks and references to Appendices

2nd Royal Inniskilling Fusiliers.

WAR DIARY for month of July 1916.

INTELLIGENCE SUMMARY.

Army Form C. 2118.

(Erase heading not required.)

Hour, Date, Place	Summary of Events and Information	Remarks and references to Appendices
1916. July 1st	Battn. was relieved by the 15th Lanc. Fus. and 16th Northumberland Fus. in trenches in THIEPVAL Subsector on night 30 June/1 July. Arrived at the BLUFF at 3.30 am, 1st July. To be in reserve to 96th Infy. Bde. during attack on THIEPVAL which commenced at 4.30 am. on 1st July. At 10 am. Bn. Hd. Qrs. and two Companies moved to JOHNSTONS POST, and one Coy to FRENCH ST at 6.55 am. One Coy remained at the BLUFF, but was sent to JOHNSTONS POST at 11.3 am. At 11.50 am. orders were sent to two Coys to attack well to the North to try and turn THIEPVAL. At 1 pm. the attack started on a two platoon frontage, but was held up by Machine Gun fire, and unable to get on. At 3.30 pm. orders were received to support the left flank of the 49th Div. (which was to attack at 4 pm.) and to fill the gap between the 49th and the 36th (Ulster) Division. This attack did not take place on the left, as one Battn. of the 49th Division only arrived up at H. 15 pm.	

WAR DIARY or INTELLIGENCE SUMMARY.

(Erase heading not required.)

Army Form C. 2118.

Hour, Date, Place	Summary of Events and Information	Remarks and references to Appendices
1916		
July 1st.	At 6.30pm the Battn. occupied the trenches on the right of the 104th Division, and remained in these trenches till relieved by HQrs 75th Bde, 25th Div., about 5.30 a.m. on 3rd July.	
" 3rd	On relief the Battn. took over dug-outs at the BLUFF, and remained there under the orders of the B.G.C. 75th Infy. Bde., until	
" 4th	9 p.m. 4th July 1916, when ordered to rejoin 96th Infy Bde in billets at WARLOY.	
	Casualties 1st to 4th July – Officers Wounded and missing – Lieut. F.J. Hutchinson. Wounded – Capt. R. & L. Holmes, Capt. F.J. Williams, 2nd Lieut. F.R.H. Bull, J.S. Newberry, L.P. Marshall, A.L.B. Wellcott, and K.L. Patterson. Other ranks Killed – 10 Wounded – 128 missing – 16. Total 154.	
" 5th	Battn. marched to HEDAUVILLE.	
" 5 – 8.	In huts at HEDAUVILLE.	
" 8th	Marched to billets in BOUZINCOURT.	
" 9th	Bivouacked near BOUZINCOURT.	

WAR DIARY
INTELLIGENCE SUMMARY

Hour, Date, Place	Summary of Events and Information	Remarks and references to Appendices
1916. July 10th. LA BOISSELLE	Battn. left BOUZINCOURT at 5 p.m. to be attached to 11th Infy Bde. at OVILLERS. Battn was ordered to attack at 9 p.m. with a view to gaining trenches and extending our line to the left of OVILLERS. Two Coys. were in front line, and two in support. The position was taken and one "Minnenwerfer" fell into our hands. At 10 p.m. one of the supporting Coys was sent up to reinforce and assist in consolidating the line gained.	
" 11th.	The enemy launched two determined Bombing attacks against our position at 3 a.m. and 9 p.m. Both attacks were repulsed, and our Lewis guns inflicted heavy loss on the enemy.	
" 12th.	Bn. held the line already gained, and consolidated the position. Considerably. Bombing activity on both sides.	
" 13th.	Battn. remained in the line. Two Coys. were ordered to attack with a view to extending our position on the 9/th Infy Bde., in conjunction with 100 men 14th H.L.I. left. The attack was successful, but owing to losses in officers and the great difficulty in recognising the ground, owing to the battered state of the trenches, the attack was carried too far, and afterwards forces back to the starting point.	
" 14th.	Bn. remained in the line. Bombing activity on both sides.	

Army Form C. 2118.

WAR DIARY
or
INTELLIGENCE SUMMARY.
(Erase heading not required.)

Instructions regarding War Diaries and Intelligence Summaries are contained in F. S. Regs., Part II. and the Staff Manual respectively. Title pages will be prepared in manuscript.

Hour, Date, Place	Summary of Events and Information	Remarks and references to Appendices
1916. July 14th	Battn. was relieved at 6 p.m. by the 2nd Manchesters 14th Bn, and withdrew to huts at BOUZINCOURT. Casualties for period 10-14 July officers - killed - Capt. C. C. Thompson 2nd Lieut. E. A. L. Walker. Wounded - 2nd Lieuts. H. F. Bell, L. Raynor Smith, L. Lundall, R. H. Boyle, and J. R. Norwood. Other ranks - killed 34 Wounded 163 missing 36 Total 233.	
" 15th.	Battn. marched to WARLOY and billeted.	
" 16th.	" " " BEAUVAL and billeted.	
" 17th.	" " " NEUVILLETTE and billeted.	
" 18th.	Remained in billets at NEUVILLETTE.	
" 19th.	Battn. marched to BLANGERMONT and billeted.	
" 20th.	" " " BERGUENEUSE and billeted.	
" 21	" " " NEDONCHELLE and billeted.	
" 21 - 25	Remained at NEDONCHELLE.	
" 26	Battn. marched to LA PUGNOY and billeted.	
" 26 - 28	Remained at LA PUGNOY.	

Army Form C. 2118.

WAR DIARY
or
INTELLIGENCE SUMMARY.

(Erase heading not required.)

Hour, Date, Place	Summary of Events and Information	Remarks and references to Appendices
1916. July 29th	Battn. marched to HEUCHIN.	
" 30 - 31	In camp at HEUCHIN. Engaged in coy training. Several Officers, N.C.O's and men were detailed to attend courses of Instruction in Bombing and Machine Gun, etc. during the latter part of the month.	

[signature] Lieut. Colonel.
Commanding 2nd Royal Inniskilling Fus.

2nd BATTALION,
ROYAL INNISKILLING
FUSILIERS.
Date 31/7/16

96th Brigade.

32nd Division.

2nd BATTALION

INNISKILLING FUSILIERS

AUGUST 1 9 1 6

D.A.G.,

The Base.

Reference your C.R. No. 140/1503, dated 29-11-16.

Duplicate War Diary of 2nd R. Innis. Fus. for month of August is forwarded herewith.

Headquarters.
6th Dec. '16.

Major General,
Commanding 32nd Division.

WAR DIARY

OF

2ND BATTALION, ROYAL INNISKILLING FUSILIERS.

From 1st August, 1916, To 31st August, 1916.

VOLUME XXV.

WAR DIARY
or
INTELLIGENCE SUMMARY.
(Erase heading not required.)

Army Form C. 2118.

2 R Irish Fus
Vol 25

Hour, Date, Place	Summary of Events and Information	Remarks and references to Appendices
1916.		
August 1 - 4.	Battalion remained in camp at HEUCHIN.	
5th.	Bn. moved to billets in TOBACCO FACTORY, BETHUNE.	
5 - 20th.	Remained in TOBACCO FACTORY, BETHUNE. Company & Battalion Training carried out.	
21st.	96th Inf. Bde. relieved 9th Inf. Bde. in the trenches in CAMBRIN Section. Bn. relieved the 14th H.L.I. in Brigade Support at MAISON ROUGE.	
21 - 24th.	Remained in Brigade Support at MAISON ROUGE.	
25	Bn. relieved the 16th Northumberland Fusiliers in the trenches in left subsection of CAMBRIN Section. 15th Lancs. on our right and 15th H.L.I. on our left.	
25 - 28	In trenches in left Sub. Section, CAMBRIN. Casualties during tour in trenches:- Wounded 2 Lieut. J.A.S. HOPKINS. Other ranks - Killed 2. Wounded 13. Missing 3.	
29	Battn. was relieved by the 16th Northumberland Fus. and withdrew to billets in Brigade Reserve at ANNEQUIN.	

WAR DIARY
or
INTELLIGENCE SUMMARY.

(Erase heading not required.)

Army Form C. 2118.

Hour, Date, Place	Summary of Events and Information	Remarks and references to Appendices
1916. August 29 – 31.	Remained in Brigade Reserve at ANNEQUIN. Working Parties of 3 Officers and 200 other ranks furnished daily for work on front line and support trenches. Several Officers, N.C.O's and men attended courses of instruction in Bombing, Lewis & Vickers Guns, Trench Mortars &c. during this month.	
31.8.16.	[signature] Lieut. Colonel Commanding 2nd Royal Inniskilling Fus.	

96th Brigade.
32nd Division.

2nd BATTALION

INNISKILLING FUSILIERS

SEPTEMBER 1916

CONFIDENTIAL.

WAR DIARY.

of

2nd. BATTALION, ROYAL INNISKILLING FUSILIERS.

From......1st September, 1916.   To.......30th September, 1916.

(Volume 25.)

2nd Royal Inniskilling Fusiliers.

WAR DIARY
INTELLIGENCE SUMMARY.

(Erase heading not required.)

Army Form C. 2118.

for month of September, 1916.

Instructions regarding War Diaries and Intelligence Summaries are contained in F.S. Regs., Part II. and the Staff Manual respectively. Title pages will be prepared in manuscript.

Hour, Date, Place	Summary of Events and Information	Remarks and references to Appendices
1916.		
1st Sept.	Battn. in Brigade Reserve at ANNEQUIN.	III
2nd Sept.	Battn. relieved the 16th Northumberland Fusrs. in trenches in left sub. section, CAMBRIN. 15th Lancs. on our right, 1st Dorsets on our left.	III
2 - 6 Sept.	Remained in trenches in left sub. section, CAMBRIN. Casualties: - Wounded - Lieut. A. C. LENDRUM, 3rd Bn. Other ranks - Wounded 9.	III
6th Sept.	Relieved by 16th Northumberland Fusrs. and withdrew. In Bde. Support at MAISON ROUGE.	III III
6 - 10 Sept.	In Brigade Support at MAISON ROUGE.	III
10th Sept.	Battn. relieved the 16th Northumberland Fusrs. in trenches in left sub. section, CAMBRIN, 15th Lancs. on our right, 16th R.I.L. on our left.	
10 - 14 Sept.	Remained in trenches in left sub. section, CAMBRIN. Casualties - tods - 2nd Lieut. A.P.R. HAINS, 3rd Connaught Rangers att. 2nd R. Innis. Fus. R.R. Killed 2, wounded H.	III III

Army Form C. 2118.

2nd Royal Inniskilling Fusiliers.

WAR DIARY
INTELLIGENCE SUMMARY.

(Erase heading not required.)

Hour, Date, Place	Summary of Events and Information	Remarks and references to Appendices
1916.		
14th Sept.	Relieved by the 16th Northumberland Fusrs and withdrew the Brigade Support at MAISON ROUGE.	nil
14th – 18th Sept.	Remained in Bde. Support at MAISON ROUGE.	nil
18th Sept.	11AM The Inf. Bde. relieved 96th Inf. Bde. in the CAMBRIN Section. Battn. relieved in Bde Support by the 15th H.L.I. and withdrew to billets in TOBACCO FACTORY, BETHUNE.	nil
18 – 26 Sept.	Remained in billets in TOBACCO FACTORY, BETHUNE. Company Training carried out. Working party of 6 officers and 150 other ranks furnished on two occasions for work on front line and support trenches.	nil
26th Sept.	96th Inf. Bde. relieved 97th Inf. Bde in the CUINCHY Section. Battn. relieved the 16th H.L.I. in the trenches in right sub-section. 15th Lancs. on our left, 15th H.L.I. and 5th Royal Scots on our right.	nil
26 – 30 Sept.	Battn. remained in trenches in right sub-section, CUINCHY.	nil

2nd Royal Inniskilling Fus.

Army Form C. 2118.

WAR DIARY
INTELLIGENCE SUMMARY
(Erase heading not required.)

Hour, Date, Place	Summary of Events and Information	Remarks and references to Appendices
1916.		
26 – 30th Sept.	Casualties during tour in trenches:—	
	Wounded:— Lieut. V. E. S. MATTOCKS.	
	Other ranks:— Killed 3, wounded 1.	nil
30th Sept.	Battn. relieved by the 16th Northumberland Fusrs. and withdrew to billets in Bde. Reserve at LE QUESNOY.	nil

J M Crawford Lieut. Colonel
Commanding 2nd Royal Inniskilling Fusrs.

-/10/16.

96th Brigade.
32nd Division.

2nd BATTALION

ROYAL INNISKILLING FUSILIERS

OCTOBER 1 9 1 6

96/32

Vol 27

CONFIDENTIAL.

WAR DIARY

of

2nd Royal Inniskilling Fusiliers.

From 1st October, 1916.   To 31st October, 1916.

VOLUME 27.

Army Form C. 2118.

WAR DIARY
INTELLIGENCE SUMMARY.
(Erase heading not required.)

Instructions regarding War Diaries and Intelligence Summaries are contained in F. S. Regs., Part II. and the Staff Manual respectively. Title pages will be prepared in manuscript.

Hour, Date, Place	Summary of Events and Information	Remarks and references to Appendices
1916.		
October 1 – 4.	Battn. remained in billets at LE QUESNOY, in Brigade Reserve.	
" 4th.	Battalion relieved the 16th Northumberland Fusiliers in the trenches in right sub-section, CUINCHY. 15th Lanc. Fus. on our left and 2nd Kings Own Yorkshire Light Infantry on our right.	
" 4 – 8	Battn. remained in trenches in the right sub-section. CUINCHY. Casualties during hour – O.R. wounded 3.	
" 8th.	Battn. relieved in trenches by the 16th Highld. Fusiliers, and withdrew to Brigade support, with Hd. Qrs. in HARLEY STREET.	
" 8 – 10	Remained in Brigade Support.	
" 10th.	96th Infy. Bde. who relieved in the line. Battn. relieved by the 2nd Yorkshire Light Infy. (97th Infy. Bde.) and the 2nd Devons. (5th Div.). Battn. withdrew to billets in ANNEZIN.	
" 10 – 15.	Remained in billets in ANNEZIN.	
" 15.	32nd Div. proceeded to rejoin the Reserve Army. Battn. marched from ANNEZIN to BEUGIN.	

Army Form C. 2118.

WAR DIARY
INTELLIGENCE SUMMARY.
(Erase heading not required.)

Instructions regarding War Diaries and Intelligence Summaries are contained in F. S. Regs., Part II. and the Staff Manual respectively. Title pages will be prepared in manuscript.

Hour, Date, Place	Summary of Events and Information	Remarks and references to Appendices
1916.		
October 16th.	Marched from BEUGIN to VILLERS BRULIN.	
" 17th.	Marched from VILLERS BRULIN to DENIER. A Tactical Exercise was carried out en route.	
" 18th.	Marched from DENIER to AMPLIER where Battn. was accommodated in huts.	
" 18 - 21	Remained at AMPLIER.	
" 21st.	Marched from AMPLIER to TOUTENCOURT. Accommodated in huts.	
" 21 - 23	Remained at TOUTENCOURT.	
" 23rd.	Marched to ALBERT, and bivouacked in the BRICKFIELDS area.	
" 23 - 26	Remained in bivouacs in the BRICKFIELDS area, ALBERT.	
" 26th.	Marched to billets in WARLOY.	
" 26 - 31	Remained in billets in WARLOY.	
" 31	Marched to billets in RUBEMPRE.	

31/10/16.

[signature] Lieut. Colonel,
Commanding 2nd Royal Inniskilling Fus.

96th Brigade
32nd Division.

2nd BATTALION

INNISKILLING FUSILIERS

NOVEMBER 1 9 1 6

WAR DIARY.

2nd.R.INNISKILLING FUSILIERS.

November 1st to 30th.1916.

WAR DIARY
INTELLIGENCE SUMMARY
(Erase heading not required.)

Army Form C. 2118.

Hour, Date, Place	Summary of Events and Information	Remarks and references to Appendices
1916.		
November 1 - 13th.	Battn. remained in billets at RUBEMPRE, and was engaged in company, Battn. and Bde. Training.	
" 13th.	Marched to WARLOY.	
" 14th.	Marched to the THIEPVAL area, and relieved the 17th Kings Royal Rifles in close support to the 117th Infty Bde, 39th Div, at ST PIERRE DIVION. The 117th Inf. Bde. was relieved by the 56th Bde, to which the Bn. then was attached in close support.	
" 14 - 17th	Bn. remained in close support to 56th Bde. at ST PIERRE DIVION, until relieved by the 4th Worcesters, 61st Div. and Bn. then marched to MAILLY MAILLET.	No casualties.
" 17/18.	Night of 17/18. in billets at MAILLY MAILLET.	
" 18th.	About 4 pm. the Battn. proceeded to the front line near BEAUMONT HAMEL, and relieved the 16th H.L.I. in the line.	
" 18 - 23	Battn. remained in the front line.	
" 23rd.	A party of 80 men of the Battn. under Capt. S.E. CLARKE, in conjunction with three coys of the 16th Lancashire Fusiliers, took part	

WAR DIARY
INTELLIGENCE SUMMARY

Army Form C. 2118.

Hour, Date, Place	Summary of Events and Information	Remarks and references to Appendices
1916.		Ref. Sheet 57D. S.E. 1/20,000. FRANCE.
November 23rd (contd)	Took part in an attack on MUNICH TRENCH. (Q.6.a.54 to Q.6.c.6.H.) with the object of receiving a party of the 97th Infy. Bde. located in dug-outs in Q.6.b.1.16. to Q.6.b.0.8., and returning with this party to our own lines. The attack commenced at 3.30pm. and succeeded in entering MUNICH TRENCH, but was unable to reach the second objective, and returned. Casualties - Officers - Killed 2/Lieut. C.F. BEVERLAND. Wounded - Capt. S.E. CLARKE, 2/Lieut. J. Mc.N. McKINSTRY and J.P. HYLAND. Other ranks - Killed 4, Wounded 42, Missing 14.	
" 24th.	Battn. was relieved by the 1st South Staffords. 91st Inf. Bde, 7th Div. and withdrew to billets in MAILLY MAILLET. Casualties during time in trenches (not including attack on 23rd) Officers - Wounded - 2/Lieut. F.C. CAIRD, (Died of Wounds) and 2nd Lieut. J.F.W. REID. Other ranks - Killed 6. Wounded 40 Missing 5.	

Army Form C. 2118.

WAR DIARY

INTELLIGENCE SUMMARY.

(Erase heading not required.)

Instructions regarding War Diaries and Intelligence Summaries are contained in F.S. Regs., Part II. and the Staff Manual respectively. Title pages will be prepared in manuscript.

Hour, Date, Place	Summary of Events and Information	Remarks and references to Appendices
1916. November 25	Battn. proceeded by buses to ORVILLE, with one company at AMPLIER.	
" 26	Marched to FIEFFES.	
" 26 - 30	Battn. remained in billets at FIEFFES, Company training carried out.	

30/11/16.

J. W. Rutherford. Lieut. Colonel,
Commanding 2nd Royal Inniskilling Fus.

96th Brigade.
32nd Division.

2nd BATTALION

ROYAL INNISKILLING FUSILIERS

DECEMBER 1 9 1 6

War Diary
of
2nd Royal Inniskilling Fusiliers
From 1st December, 1916
To 31st December, 1916.

Volume - XXIX

Army Form C. 2118.

WAR DIARY
or
INTELLIGENCE SUMMARY.
(Erase heading not required.)

29.H

Place	Date	Hour	Summary of Events and Information	Remarks and references to Appendices
	1916. 1st to 31st Dec.		Battalion remained in billets at FIEFFES, and was engaged in Company, Battalion and Brigade Training, and exercises in musketry. Several officers, N.C.O's and men were detailed to attend courses of Instruction in Bombing, Bayonet Fighting, Lewis Gun, Trench Mortars etc., during the month. The Battalion was inspected by the G.O.C. V Corps on the 5th instant, on a Brigade Ceremonial Parade. The Fifth Army Commander inspected Companies at Training on the 18th instant. Sports were indulged in during the afternoons and competitions in football, boxing, running, bayonet fighting etc. were carried out under Brigade and Divisional arrangements, in which the Battalion figured very creditably.	

31.12.16

J.W. Maxwell Lieut. Colonel,
Commanding 2nd Royal Inniskilling Fusiliers.

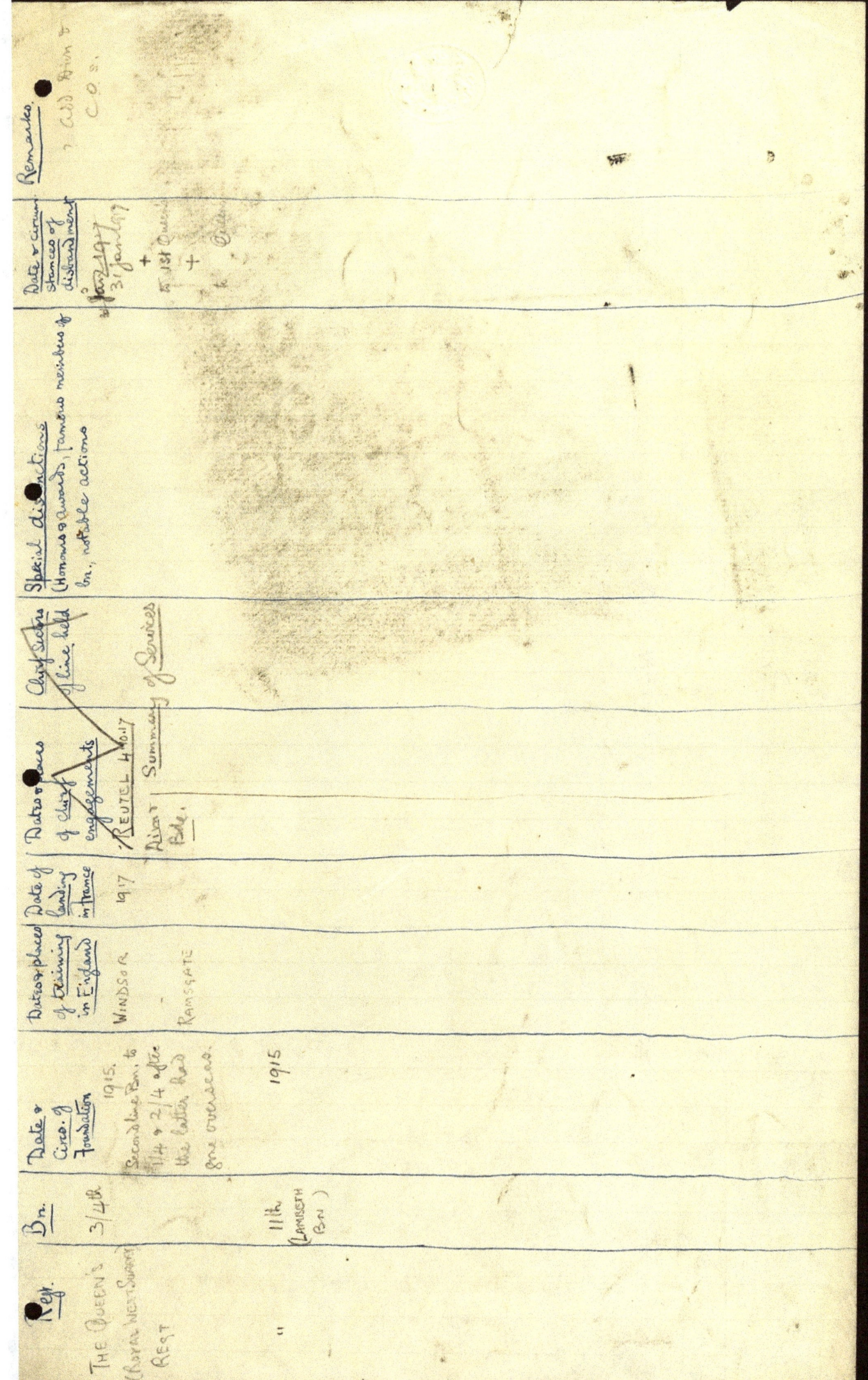

Regt.	Bn.	Date & Circs. of Foundation	Dates & places of training in England	Date of landing in France	Dates & places of chief engagements	Chief sectors of line held	Special distinctions (Honours & awards, famous members of Bn., notable actions	Date & circumstances of disbandment	Remarks
THE QUEEN'S (ROYAL WEST SURREY) REGT	3/4th	1915. Second line Bn, to 1/4 & 2/4 after the latter had gone overseas.	WINDSOR – RAMSGATE	1917	REUTEL 4 Nov 17 Summary of services Avion Pole.			5 Nov 1917 31 Jan 1919 + 51st Queen's to Queen's	? add Bm to C.O.S.
"	11th (Lambeth Bn.)	1915							

WAR DIARY
INTELLIGENCE SUMMARY.
(Erase heading not required.)

Army Form C. 2118.

Place	Date	Hour	Summary of Events and Information	Remarks and references to Appendices
	1914. Jan.			
	1-6.		Battalion remained in Billets in FIEFFES and was engaged in Company and Battalion Training, and exercised in Musketry.	
	6		Battalion marched RAINCHEVAL.	
	7		Battalion marched to LOUVENCOURT.	
	7-14		Battalion remained in Billets in LOUVENCOURT. Three companies were engaged in working parties. One company was engaged in Company Training.	
	14		Battalion (less 1 Coy) moved to Billets in COURCELLES. A Company were accommodated in dug-outs in HITTITE and PAPIN Trenches, in support to the 2/5th Suff. Scots.	
	14-16.		Battalion remained in Brigade Reserve in Billets in COURCELLES.	
	16.		Battalion relieved the 16th Northumberland Fusiliers in the Left Sub-Sector (C.4). 9th Royal Welsh Fusiliers on our left and 15th Lancashire Fusiliers on our right.	
	16-18		Battalion remained in Trenches in the left sub sector.	
	18		Battalion relieved in Trenches by the 9th Cheshire Regiment. 8th Infy. Brigade. 3rd Division and withdrew to Billets in COURCELLES. Casualties during tour - Nil.	
	19		D Company relieved the 5/6th Royal Scots at the White City, and remained in	

Army Form C. 2118.

WAR DIARY

INTELLIGENCE SUMMARY.

(Erase heading not required.)

Instructions regarding War Diaries and Intelligence Summaries are contained in F. S. Regs., Part II and the Staff Manual respectively. Title pages will be prepared in manuscript.

Place	Date	Hour	Summary of Events and Information	Remarks and references to Appendices
HEBUTERNE	1917 January 18-21		Battalion remained in Billets in COURCELLES.	
	21		Battalion marched to MAILLY MAILLET.	
	21-22		Remained in Billets in MAILLY-MAILLET.	
	22-3		Battalion relieved the 15th Lancashire Fusiliers in C.3 left sub-Sector. 9th Royal Welsh Fusiliers on our left and 16th Lancashire Fusiliers on our right. D Company were relieved at K.28.C.6 by A Company of the 15th Highland Light Infantry and regained Battalion in left sub-sector K.28.830.15, and relieved A Company of the 15th Lancashire Fusiliers.	
	23-25		Battalion remained in trenches in C.3 left sub sector.	
	25		Battalion relieved in trenches by 15th Lancashire Fusiliers and withdrew to Billets in MAILLY-MAILLET. Casualties during tour – 2 O.R. slightly wounded.	
	25-26		Battalion remained in Billets in MAILLY-MAILLET.	
	26-29		Battalion relieved the 16th Lancashire Fusiliers in the Right Sub sector. 16th Northumberland Fusiliers on our left and 1st ------ on our right.	
	29-31		Battalion remained in trenches in Right Sub sector. Casualties up to date 1 O.R. killed. 3 O.R. wounded.	Map Reference 1/10,000 57D S.E.

J. W. R. ------ Major.
Commanding 2nd Royal Inniskilling Fusiliers

Confidential

War Diary

of

2nd. Royal Inniskilling Fusiliers.

From 1st February 1917.   To 28th February 1917.

Volume XXXI.

[signature], Lieut Colonel.
Commanding 2nd Royal Inniskilling Fusiliers

Army Form C. 2118.

WAR DIARY
INTELLIGENCE SUMMARY.
(Erase heading not required.)

Vol 31

Instructions regarding War Diaries and Intelligence Summaries are contained in F. S. Regs., Part II. and the Staff Manual respectively. Title pages will be prepared in manuscript.

Place	Date	Hour	Summary of Events and Information	Remarks and references to Appendices
In the field	July 1		Battalion, less 2 Companies, were relieved in Trenches (G.3). left sub sector by the 10th Manchester Regiment and withdrew to Billets in BERTRANCOURT. Casualties during tour - 1 other rank killed; 5 other ranks wounded.	nil
	1		"A" and "B" Companies marched to Trenches at Q.14.a.8.8. and were accommodated in dugouts and were engaged in working parties.	nil
	1-5		Battalion, less 2 Companies, remained in Billets in BERTRANCOURT and were engaged in working parties.	nil
	5		Battalion, less 2 Companies, marched to MAILLY-MAILLET and took over Billets vacated by 15th Lancashire Fusiliers.	nil
	12		"A" and "B" Companies were relieved off working parties and rejoined Battalion in Billets in MAILLY-MAILLET.	nil
	5-13		Battalion remained in Billets in MAILLY-MAILLET, and were engaged in working parties. "B" Company were engaged in Company and Platoon Training.	nil
	13		Battalion marched to BEAUMONT-HAMEL and were attached to 99th Infantry Brigade	nil
	14		Battalion ceased to be attached to 99th Infantry Brigade and withdrew to Billets in BERTRANCOURT. Casualties during Tour - 1 other wounded.	nil
	15		Battalion marched to Billets in HARPONVILLE	nil
	16		Battalion marched to Billets in MIRVAUX	nil
	16-17		Battalion became incorporated in the Fourth Army and Reinforcement Troops.	nil
	17		Battalion marched to Billets in TALMAS	nil

WAR DIARY
INTELLIGENCE SUMMARY.
(Erase heading not required.)

Army Form C. 2118.

Place	Date 1917	Hour	Summary of Events and Information	Remarks and references to Appendices
In the field	July 19		Battalion remained in billets in TALMAS. Companies were at the disposal of Company Commanders and practised extended order advancing.	—
	20.		Battalion marched to billets in RIVERY.	—
	21.		Battalion marched to billets in DOMART and received a reinforcement of 1 Officer and 129 other ranks.	—
	22-23.		Battalion remained in billets in DOMART	—
	25.		Battalion marched to billets in BEAUFORT	—
	25-26		Battalion remained in billets in BEAUFORT	—
	27.		Battalion marched to trenches in left sub-sector, and relieved the 140th Infantry Regiment of the 27th (French) Division. Three companies in front line and one company in reserve. 14th Gloucester Regiment on our left and 15th Lancashire Fusiliers on our right. In 24-26th and 16th Lancashire Fusiliers on our right since night of 26th.	—
	24-28		Battalion remained in trenches in left sub-sector. "A" Company moving into the front line on night of 26th.	—
	28		Battalion relieved in trenches in left sub-sector by the 15th Lancashire Fusiliers and withdrew to intermediate line in Brigade support. Casualties during tour — 2 officers wounded, 1 officer wounded and prisoner of war, 30 other ranks killed, 40 other ranks wounded.	—

G. Maughd [?]
Lieut Colonel
Commanding 2nd Royal Inniskilling Fusiliers.

WAR DIARY.

of

2nd Bn. Royal Inniskilling Fusiliers.

From 1st March 1917.   To 31st March 1917.

Vol. 32.

Confidential.

War Diary

-of-

2nd Royal Inniskilling Fus.

From 1st. March 1914.

To 31st March 1914.

Volume XXXII.

G. Dawson Lieut Colonel
Commdg. 2nd Royal Inniskilling Fusiliers.

Army Form C. 2118.

WAR DIARY
or
INTELLIGENCE SUMMARY.
(Erase heading not required.)

Instructions regarding War Diaries and Intelligence Summaries are contained in F. S. Regs., Part II. and the Staff Manual respectively. Title pages will be prepared in manuscript.

Place	Date 1917	Hour	Summary of Events and Information	Remarks and references to Appendices
	Mar 1		Battalion remained in intermediate line in Brigade Support	
	2		Battalion relieved in trenches by the 11th Border Regiment, 4th Infantry Brigade and withdrew to billets in LE QUESNEL	
	2-8		Battalion remained in billets in LE QUESNEL. Battalion and company training carried out. Battalion also engaged in working parties.	
	8-9		Battalion relieved 5/6th Royal Scots in right sub sector. 2nd Battalion 123rd Regiment, 35th Division (French) on our right and 16th Lancashire Fusiliers on our left	
	11-12		Battalion relieved in right sub sector by 16th Northumberland Fusiliers and 15th Lancashire Fusiliers. Two platoons of A Company billeted in BOUCHOIR and two accommodated in dugouts in LABYRINTH. C Company in dugouts at OUVRAGE PIERRET. Headquarters, Band & B Company in dugouts in LE QUESNOY	
	14-15		Battalion relieved 16th Northumberland Fusiliers in right sub sector. B, D and A Companies in front line. C Company in support with Battalion Headquarters at AUSTERLITZ. 2nd Battalion 123rd Regiment, 35th Division (French) on our right, 16th Lancashire Fusiliers on our left.	
	16		Battalion received orders to send out patrols in conjunction with the French. Orders cancelled owing to fog lifting.	
	17		Battalion Headquarters moved to D Company's Headquarters in line. At 9am trench advanced on our right and met with no opposition. Patrols were sent out to keep in touch with 358th French Regiment on right. 16th Northumberland Fusiliers relieved us on right. Battalion dug a trench now in no man's land to keep in touch with 16th Northumberland Fusiliers Battalion advanced at 6 p.m. and took up an outpost position in the GOYENCOURT - PARVILLERS Road just East of DAMERY. 16th Lancashire Fusiliers on left and 30 yds French Regiment on right. Distribution of Companies. D Company left at BOIS - PAYEN. A Company Centre. C Right - B	

WAR DIARY
or
INTELLIGENCE SUMMARY.

(Erase heading not required.)

Army Form C. 2118.

Instructions regarding War Diaries and Intelligence Summaries are contained in F. S. Regs., Part II and the Staff Manual respectively. Title pages will be prepared in manuscript.

Place	Date 1917	Hour	Summary of Events and Information	Remarks and references to Appendices
	Mar 18	9 am	Battalion advanced to line FRESNOY LES ROYE - HATTENCOURT, touch being maintained with 6th Lancashire fusiliers on left and 20th French Regiment on right. Battalion took up position on the road running North - South just East of FRESNOY. Patrols went out as far as BOIS LATTES, string points being established along this line. Battalion advanced to CREMERY at 4 pm and bivouacked and became Battalion in Brigade reserve.	* Ref. Map. 66 N + 66 D N.W. Squares G33v Ref. Map. 66 D 1/40000
	19		Battalion advanced to NESLE. Battalion in support and bivouacked at I.25.d.4.y. @ At 4pm Battalion moved to BECQUINCOURT via QUIQUERY and billeted. Battalion in Brigade reserve.	
	20		"B" and "D" companies moved to Billets in HOMBLEUX.	
	20-23		Battalion less 2 companies remained in Billets in BECQUINCOURT, in Brigade Reserve.	
	23		Battalion marched to TOULLE relieving the 16th Lancashire Fusiliers in the TOULLE - MATIGNY line. "A" "C" and "B" companies in line and "A" company in support. 1st Horse Regiment 17th Infantry Brigade on our left, and 91st Regiment 19th Division (French) on our right, and later 22nd Regiment 28th Division (French). Battalion engaged in digging a line of trenches and putting some in a state of defence. Troops being acting as a covering force, they having already established outposts on the line Germaine - BEAUVOIS.	
	28		Battalion established an outpost at MARGERE FARM.	
	28-31		Battalion remained in TOULLE and became Battalion in Divisional Reserve on the 28th.	
	31	10 pm	Battalion moved to FORESTE.	

H. Crawford
Lieut Colonel
Commanding 2nd Royal Inniskilling Fusiliers

Sept 6 22
Sept 13 9
Sept 27 9

CONFIDENTIAL.

WAR DIARY.

OF

2nd ROYAL INNISKILLING FUSILIERS.

From 1st April 1917.   To 30th April 1917.

Vol. xxxiii

Confidential

War Diary

of

2nd Royal Inniskilling Fusiliers

From 1st April 1917.   To 30th April 1917.

Volume XXXIII.

J M Crawford Lieut Colonel
Commanding 2nd Royal Inniskilling Fusiliers

WAR DIARY
INTELLIGENCE SUMMARY

Army Form C. 2118.

(Erase heading not required.)

Hour, Date, Place	Summary of Events and Information	Remarks and References to Appendices
April 1917	1. Battalion in billets at FORESTE. Received orders at 5 a.m. to move to CHATEAU DE POMERY. Battalion moved off at 6 a.m. arriving at destination at 8.30 a.m. where it remained until forming up for attack on SAVY WOOD and word in S.26.B. Battalion received orders at 11.30 a.m. to advance at 1.30 p.m. Battalion advances to SAVY in artillery formation, under hostile artillery fire. Battalion formed up and advanced at 3 p.m. in extended order. "C" "B" and "D" Companies in front line and "A" Company in support. Battalion met with heavy enemy artillery and machine gun fire. Battalion entered wood in S.26.B. at 3.30 p.m. when the artillery barrage lifted. Battalion renewed final objective at 3.40 p.m. and commenced consolidating, being practically unopposed throughout. "A" Company sent forward to reinforce front line. Casualties — Officer 1 killed, 10 wounded, other ranks 31, wounded 107, missing 3. Officer casualties, Kent J.A. Gallion 4th R. Irish Regiment killed, Captain F.A. Moodey, 3rd Batt Kenton R.C. London, Kent A.E.K. Geoghegan 3rd B. (Chan of Ireland 13.4.17) Kent E.I. Burke 4th R. Irish Rgrs. 12th Bn, Kent J.R. A'Henry 4th M. Fus, Lieut. C.E. Baker, 10th Bn, ... Kent D.J. Byrne 4th Connaught Rangers. Kent J. Barron 4th R. Irish Regiment and Rev. J. Knighton R.C. chaplain, wounded.	Reference Sheet 62.B. 1/40,000. 1st Edition. 17th Highland Light Infantry 97th Infantry Brigade on right. 15th Lancashire Fusiliers on left.
	2) In conjunction with attack of 97th Infantry Brigade on MOLNON FRANCILLY, SILENCY and the new forward of the	nil

WAR DIARY or INTELLIGENCE SUMMARY

Army Form C. 2118.

(Erase heading not required.)

Instructions regarding War Diaries and Intelligence Summaries are contained in F. S. Regs., Part II and the Staff Manual respectively. Title pages will be prepared in manuscript.

Place	Date 1917	Hour	Summary of Events and Information	Remarks and references to Appendices
	April 2		went forward of the 16th Northumberland Fusiliers on our left. Battalion advanced to position and took up a line and connected from Junction point X22 in S.26.B. to S.21.D.1.5. Touch being maintained with 16th Northum. Fusiliers 28' A' and 'B' Coys and in front. 'C' Company in support in wood. Battalion Head-quarters at S.26.B.6.2. Battalion in touch with 109th Regiment 25th French Division on Right. En = Officer casualties: Went. L.Y.P. Battn. 3rd Bn. Wounded.	Reference Sheet 62.B. 1/40,000 1st Edition
	3		In conjunction with attack of French on GRUGIES D'ALLON and L'EPINE DE DALLON Battalion advanced its Right to cross roads in S.27.B. and consolidated.	
	4		Battalion engaged in consolidating position taken up, and digging a continuous trench, with strong posts at intervals. French moved forward to front the trench with their left flank at about S.22.D.4.5. And 16th Northumberland Fusiliers on left. Battalion was ordered to establish an outpost line on the highest ground between S.21.D.6.8. and the road about S.27.B.1.9. This was done and full arrangements for keeping maintained touch between our troops by means of patrols	
			on Right and the 16th Northumberland Fusiliers on Left.	
	5		Position unchanged. Company engaged in work in line and wiring	
	6		Position unchanged. Company continued same work	
	7		Position unchanged. Company continued work on lines and wiring	
	8		Position unchanged. Company continued work on line and wiring	
	9		Position unchanged. Company continued work on line and wiring	
	10		Position unchanged. D Company established in two strong points at S.22.B.4.5 and S.22.C.2.5.	Reference 62.B. WWI Survey Sheet No.2. 1/20,000

WAR DIARY or INTELLIGENCE SUMMARY

Army Form C. 2118.

(Erase heading not required.)

Instructions regarding War Diaries and Intelligence Summaries are contained in F. S. Regs., Part II. and the Staff Manual respectively. Title pages will be prepared in manuscript.

Place	Date 1917	Hour	Summary of Events and Information	Remarks and references to Appendices
	April 11		Battalion relieved on line by 16th Lancashire Fusiliers and withdrew to SAVY, where it remained in Brigade Reserve. Capt Asher 16th Northumberland Fusiliers in command of Battalion. Lieutenant Colonel Beaufort D.S.O. Sick.	62 C 1/40,000 Sheet 1.
	12		Battalion relieved by 2nd Manchester Regiment 14th Infantry Brigade and withdrew to BEAUVOIS and billeted. Battalion in Divisional Reserve. Lieutenant Colonel Beaufort resumed Command of Battalion. Casualties - other ranks Killed 2, wounded 3.	Reference Sheet 62 C 1/40,000 Not Shown
	13		BEAUVOIS	
	14		BEAUVOIS. Received orders at 9am. to move to ATILLY and to be in support to an attack by 97th Infantry Brigade. On road received order to proceed to ETREILLERS, and later move to BIHECOURT at GERMAINE.	
GERMAINE	15		Battalion moved to HOLNON, where it remained in Brigade Reserve.	
HOLNON	16			
HOLNON	17		Battalion engaged in digging a line of resistance (or outpost line) from SEPT S.6.d.7.5 exclusive to read at M.36 Central thence to north east corner of TWIN COPSE) on the line M.33.B.4.0. to read at S.3.B.9.9. Work continued on line of resistance. Battalion relieved 16th Lancashire Fusiliers in the outpost line from SEPT S.6.d.7.5 exclusive to read at M.36 Central thence to North East corner of TWIN COPSE, 15th West and Derby Regiment, 105th Infantry Brigade 35th Division on left. 17th Highland Light Infantry, 19th Infantry Brigade on Right. A Company, 16th Northumberland Fusiliers	Reference Sheet 62.B. S.W. Section 2A 1/40,000

WAR DIARY or INTELLIGENCE SUMMARY

Army Form C. 2118.

Place	Date	Hour	Summary of Events and Information	Remarks and references to Appendices
	April 18		Attached for duty. Disposition of Companies: A Company 16th Northumberland Fusiliers left; B and C Company on the right and D Company in support. Major Fisher 16th Northumberland Fusiliers in command of Battalion (Colonel Graupra D.S.O. sick) to Transport lines.	Reference 62 C. SW 1/2, 2/2. (?) Reference 62 C. 1/40,000 Edition.
	19		Outpost line heavily shelled throughout day. Battalion headquarters at FYNET.	
	20		Battalion relieved in line by 3/5th Gloucester Regiment 183rd Infantry Brigade, 61st Division and proceeded to BECC BEAUVOIS, being part of Brigade Divisional Reserve.	Reference Sheet 66 B. 1/40,000 Edition.
	21		Battalion relieved by 2/7th Worcesters 61st Division, and marched to CROIX MOLIGNAUX and X and Y billeted areas in Corps Reserve.	
	22-30		CROIX MOLIGNAUX and Y. Battalion engaged in Company training and working parties.	

Commanding 2/6th Royal Innes Killing Fusiliers

WAR DIARY or INTELLIGENCE SUMMARY

Army Form C. 2118.

Place	Date	Hour	Summary of Events and Information	Remarks and references to Appendices
1917.	May 1		Battalion remained in Billets in CROIX MOLIGNAUX and Y. The Battalion in conjunction with other units of the 96th Infantry Brigade was inspected by G.O.C. 32nd Division who congratulated the Commanding Officer on the smart appearance of men and transport.	
	2.		Battalion remained in Billets in CROIX MOLIGNAUX and Y. and was engaged in working parties and training.	
	3.		Battalion remained in Billets in CROIX MOLIGNAUX and Y. 96th Infantry Brigade inspected by Corps Commander.	
	4.		Battalion remained in Billets in CROIX MOLIGNAUX and Y. Captain S.A. MacDonell, D.S.O., 1st K.O.Y.L.I. joined Battalion and took over the duties of Temporary Second-in-Command.	
	5-6.		Battalion remained in Billets in CROIX MOLIGNAUX and Y. and was engaged in training and working parties.	
	7.		Battalion remained in Billets in CROIX MOLIGNAUX and Y. Lieut. Colonel J.W. Crawford, D.S.O., proceeded to England on Medical Grounds. Captain S.A. MacDonell D.S.O., took over Command of Battalion.	
	8-12.		Battalion remained in Billets in CROIX MOLIGNAUX and Y. and was engaged in training and working parties.	
	13.		Battalion remained in Billets in CROIX MOLIGNAUX and Y. Major E.A. Rigg, D.S.O., 2nd K.O.Y.L.I. joined Battalion for duty, and took over Command of the Battalion.	
	14.		Battalion remained in Billets in CROIX MOLIGNAUX and Y. Battalion marched to ENNEMAIN and took part in a Brigade Tactical Scheme.	
	15.		Battalion remained in Billets in CROIX MOLIGNAUX and Y. Battalion held a very successful sports meeting at which a great many competitors from different units and Brigade Headquarters took part.	
	16.		Battalion marched to OMIECOURT and billeted there for the night.	

WAR DIARY
INTELLIGENCE SUMMARY

(Erase heading not required.)

Army Form C. 2118.

Place	Date	Hour	Summary of Events and Information	Remarks and references to Appendices
1917	May 17		Battalion marched to CAIX.	Reference sheet 66D 1/40,000
	18		Battalion remained in Billets in CAIX and was engaged in constructing Rifle Range, Bombing Grenade and Bayonet fighting Course.	
	19-23		Battalion remained in Billets in CAIX and was engaged in training.	Reference Sheet 66 E N E CHAULNES 66D N.W. Parts
	24		Battalion took part in a Practice Exercise carried out by the 96th Infantry Brigade over the old English trenches opposite CHAULNES.	
	25		Battalion remained in Billets in CAIX. Companies were at the disposal of Company Commanders for kit inspection, interior economy.	
	26		Battalion remained in Billets in CAIX. Battalion took part in a Brigade Sports Meeting, and being very successful, it scored the largest number of prizes at the meeting. A general invitation was issued to the inhabitants of the village, of which the Mayor and a large number of the population availed themselves of the opportunity of witnessing an interesting and excellent sports meeting.	
	27-28		Battalion remained in Billets in CAIX and was engaged in training.	
	29		Battalion remained in Billets in CAIX. The officers of the Battalion in conjunction with those of Brigade Headquarters and 16th Lancashire Fusiliers gave a musical entertainment in the Theatre, to which the Mayor and civil population were invited.	
	30		Battalion remained in Billets in CAIX and was engaged in training. "C" Company moved to Billets in GUILLAUCOURT for the purpose of finding Working parties at Nissen Huts for use of 96th Infantry Brigade to another area.	
	31		During the period the Battalion was resting, special attention was paid to Musketry. Bore shooting competitions by Companies were arranged and carried out each afternoon.	

NOTE:

Commanding 2nd Royal Inniskilling Fusiliers

Reference sheet 66 D 1/40,000

Confidential

War Diary

of

2nd Batt Royal Inniskilling Fusiliers

From 1st June 1917   To 30th June 1917

Volume XXXV

J H MacDonald Major

Commanding 2nd Royal Inniskilling Fus.

WAR DIARY
INTELLIGENCE SUMMARY.
(Erase heading not required.)

Army Form C. 2118.

2 R Munich Fus

Hour, Date, Place	Summary of Events and Information	Remarks and references to Appendices
1917 June 1st	32nd Division having received orders to join XIV Corps and Army Battalion less C Coy proceeded by rail to CASTRE at which place they detrained and marched to BLEU where they billeted. C Coy requiring about 11:30 p.m. Brigade in support to II ANZAC Corps for operations at MESSINES	SHEET 5&D 1/40,000 9th 4th HAZEBROUCK SHEET 36A & 37A 1/100,000 ED 2 and 27 1/100,000
2nd 15.11th.	Remained in billets at BLEU. Brigade and Battalion route marches and training carried out. Special attention being paid to musketry	J.B.Lee
12th	Battalion marched to EECKE area and were billeted at WAGENBRUGE Division from XV Corps	SHEET 9A N7 1/40,000 J.B.Lee
13th	Battalion marched to WORMHOUDT and billeted	J.B. 4th SHEET 27 1/40,000 J.B.Lee
14th	Remained in billets at WORMHOUDT. Coys engaged in intown economy and judging distance	J.B.Lee
15th	Battalion marched to UXEM and billeted	J.B.Lee SHEETS 27 - 19 1/40,000
16th	Remained in billets at UXEM. Battalion congratulated by G O C 96th Infantry Brigade on their fine marching of day previous	J.B.Lee
18th	Battalion less 1st Line Transport marched to LEFFRINCKHOUCKE platoon for entrainment to COXYDE and thence march to BADOR CAMP. Transport proceeded by road	SHEETS 19. 11. 12 1/40,000 J.B.Lee
19th	Battalion marched to support line A Sub sector relieving 15th Lancashire Fusiliers and were responsible for the defence of the coast from AEOLIENNE road enclosure to the canal. Battalion were billeted in cellars on sea front NIEUPORT-LES BAINS. Casualties during tour Other Ranks 1 killed 3 wounded.	J.B.Lee

Army Form C. 2118.

WAR DIARY
or
INTELLIGENCE SUMMARY
(Erase heading not required.)

Instructions regarding War Diaries and Intelligence Summaries are contained in F.S. Regs., Part II. and the Staff Manual respectively. Title pages will be prepared in manuscript.

Place	Date	Hour	Summary of Events and Information	Remarks and references to Appendices
1917	June 22nd		Battalion relieved in support line A sub-section by 1st Cameron Highlanders 1st Brigade 1st Division and marched to JEAN-BART camp where they billeted for the night	9.17a. 9.17m.
	23rd		Battalion marched to GHYVELDE area and billeted	SHEETS 11.5 & 11.5.M
	24.5.30a		Battalion in billets at GHYVELDE. Section, Platoon and Company Training carried out. Special attention being paid to musketry and Bayonet fighting. Battalion engaged in digging trenches etc, for practice purposes for forthcoming operations. Practice attacks under Battalion and Company arrangements carried out.	1/20000 9.17m.

J. H. Macdonald Major
Commanding 2nd Royal Inniskilling Fusiliers

WAR DIARY

OF

2nd ROYAL INNISKILLING FUSILIERS.

JULY, 1917.

WAR DIARY
or
INTELLIGENCE SUMMARY.

Army Form C. 2118.

Place	Date	Hour	Summary of Events and Information	Remarks and references to Appendices
	July 1916 3rd		Battalion in billets at GHYVELDE. Brigade Tactical exercise being carried out. Moved to forward area to march south. B and C Coys to RIBAILLET HQ Coy A and C Coys to JEANNIOT Camp	BELGIUM, FRANCE SHEET 19 0 22 SHEET 11 X 13.a
	4th			
	5th		Marched to the line in relief of 3/6th Royal Scots 144th Bde in the right sub-sector ST GEORGES sector 2 Coys but front line and 2 in support at NIEUPORT. 144th Belgians 3rd Division on our right and 16th Lancashires Fusiliers on our left (on the night of the 9th and 11th Belgium were relieved by the 9th Belgians of the same Regiment) This is the most pectilier portion of the line the Battalion has ever held the majority of the Sub-sector being Under water and the surrounding country absolutely flat.	NIEUPORT SHEET 12 M 27 & 7D M 34 a & b
	15th		Battalion relieved in the line by the 1/5th K.O.Y.L.I 49th Division and marched to billets at COXYDE. During the period on the trenches the Headquarters of 15 Coy received a direct hit from a 5.9 Howitzer during a bombardment by the enemy turning 1 Officer and 3 Other Ranks, the Officer and two Other Ranks were extricated alive but the other man was killed. Total casualties during tour of duty 6 Other Ranks killed 4 O Ranks wounded. One Officer 2/Lieut T H Bird wounded slightly.	SHEET 11 X 13 a
	19th		Marched to OOST DUNKIRK and came under the O.C. 257 Tunnelling Coy R E for work. A and E Coy at NIEUPORT- Hd qrs. B and D Coys at OOST DUNKIRK. Battalion in Divisional Reserve to 49th Division	SHEET 11 X 4.6
	20th			
	26th		Relieved by 2nd K.O.Y.L.I 97th Bde and marched to BRAY-DUNES Less B and D Coys who remained at work under 257 Tunnelling Coy R.E. till 8.30 p.m billeting at COXYDE night of 26/27th and rejoined Battalion on 27th inst – Casualties whilst attached to R.E. 1 O Rank killed 3 O Ranks wounded. – 1 Officer and 243 O Ranks (James) Officer 2/Lieut. A H Semple	SHEET 19 D.9 a

Army Form C. 2118.

WAR DIARY
or
INTELLIGENCE SUMMARY.
(Erase heading not required.)

Instructions regarding War Diaries and Intelligence Summaries are contained in F. S. Regs., Part II. and the Staff Manual respectively. Title pages will be prepared in manuscript.

Place	Date	Hour	Summary of Events and Information	Remarks and references to Appendices
	July 27/31		Battalion in billets at BRAY-DUNES (6 Comps) Companies engaged in various demonstrations and building new Rifle Range.	9.12
	July 26th		(Continued) "Gassed". Caused by Gas shell used by the enemy for the 1st time and very difficult to detect. It affected the eyes, the some cases causing temporary blindness, as well as causing temporary loss of speech, in many cases the effect only became apparent after the lapse of a few days.	
	July 27/31		Battalion billeted in BRAY/DUNES (6 Camps). Companies engaged in various demonstrations, and building new Rifle Range.	9.12

Owen H. Henderson Lt.Col.

— Confidential —

War Diary

of

2nd Batt. Royal Inniskilling Fusiliers

From 1st August 1917   To. 31st August 1917

Volume XXXVII.

signature Riggs

Lieut-Colonel
Commanding 2nd Royal Inniskilling Fus.

Army Form C. 2118.

WAR DIARY
or
INTELLIGENCE SUMMARY.

(Erase heading not required.)

2 R. Irish Fus
Vol 3 7

Place	Date	Hour	Summary of Events and Information	Remarks and references to Appendices
1917	Aug 1st		Battalion relieved the 1/6th West Yorkshire Regiment 146th Infantry Brigade in the Right Sub-Sector St George's Sector on the night of 1st/2nd August "B" and "D" Coys in line with "A" and "C" Coys in support at MAISON BLANCHE. 3rd Belgian Division on our right and the 16th Lancashire Fusiliers on our left.	RIR M.R. Bassum 12 B.1.9
"	3-4		16th Northumberland Fusiliers relieved the 16th Lancashire Fusiliers on our left on the night of 3rd/4th August.	RIR
"	4		Battalion relieved in the line on the night of 4th/5th August by the 15th Lancashire Fusiliers and withdrew to billets in RIBAILLET Camp. Casualties during tour, 1 OR wounded.	RIR Oost-Dunkirk sheet 11. R 35 d.
"	5-13		Battalion remained in billets in RIBAILLET CAMP and was employed on working parties in the line	RIR
"	14		Battalion in billets in RIBAILLET CAMP. Camp heavily bombarded with "Gas" and "H.E." Shells from 12 Midnight till 4-30 am on morning of 15th. Our casualties were very small owing to the promptness with which the men put on their Box Respirators and to the fact that the Camp was cleared. It is interesting to note that the effect of the gas was very local the Companies only went about 400 yards from the Camp and found that there was no need for Box Respirators at all. A direct hit was obtained on Battalion Head Quarters Mess hut but no one was injured. Casualties during bombardment :— Major J.H. Macdonnell D.S.O.	RIR

WAR DIARY or INTELLIGENCE SUMMARY.

Army Form C. 2118.

Place	Date	Hour	Summary of Events and Information	Remarks and references to Appendices
1917	Aug 14		Lieut J. Hamilton, 3 O.R. wounded (gassed) 1 O.R. died of wounds (gas) 3 O.R. wounded and 1 O.R. died of wounds. N.B:- Two days after the Battalion was relieved, the camp was again shelled and has now been evacuated.	MR
"	16-17		Battalion in billets in RIBAILLET CAMP. 4th Suffolk Regiment	MR
"	17		Battalion relieved by 2nd Argyle and Sutherland Highlanders SHEET II.	MR
			98th Infantry Brigade and withdrew to COXYDE and bivouacked for the night.	
			Total casualties during period 5.8 – 17.8:—	
			Officers wounded (gas) - 2	
			O.R. " " - 14	
			O.R. Died of wounds " - 5	
			O.R. Killed - 5	
			O.R. wounded - 14	
			O.R. Died of wounds - 5	
"	18		Battalion marched to BRAY DUNES and billeted in "C" Camp.	MR SHEET
"	18-29		Battalion remained in billets in "C" Camp BRAY DUNES and was engaged in Company, Platoon and Specialist training	MR

WAR DIARY
or
INTELLIGENCE SUMMARY.
(Erase heading not required.)

Army Form C. 2118.

Instructions regarding War Diaries and Intelligence Summaries are contained in F. S. Regs., Part II. and the Staff Manual respectively. Title pages will be prepared in manuscript.

Place	Date	Hour	Summary of Events and Information	Remarks and references to Appendices
1917	Aug 18-29		Musketry was also carried out daily	9RR SHEET II
	"29		Battalion marched to COXYDE and billets in CANADA CAMP (JEAN10TT) and were in Divisional Reserve	9RR *13a.
	29-31		Battalion remained in billets in CANADA CAMP COXYDE, and companies were engaged in training of Specialists	9RR.

G.A. Rees, Lieut-Colonel,
Commanding 2nd Royal Inniskilling Fusiliers

Army Form C. 2118.

WAR DIARY
or
INTELLIGENCE SUMMARY.
(Erase heading not required.)

Place	Date	Hour	Summary of Events and Information	Remarks and references to Appendices
	Sept 1917 contd		Battalion in Billets in CANADA CAMP (JEANNIOT) COXYDE. Coy training and Traning of Specialists carried out. Brigade Sports were carried out in which the Battalion did very well - winning the 100 yds. 1/2 mile. Relay Race and much more - and in Tug of War. Inter-Division Revisions and Football (association) an Officers Rugby team was formed but only managed to arrange for two matches - winning 1 to the V. remainder of Brigade. XV won 1 to 5. Points out V. 15th & 16th Lancs. 0-8 points to nil. Working parties were found daily for work under the R.E. or the Y.S.E.R. Cire	R.W.R.
	12th - 13th		Battalion relieved 2nd Manchester Regiment 6/7. 14th Brigade and took over the defences of NIEUPORT and PRESQUILE high NIEUPORT special No. 3.	
	16th - 17th		Battalion relieved the 16th Northumberland Fusiliers in the Right Sub-Sector of the LOMBARTZYDE Sector "A" & "E" (being composite companies had one Coy frontage) and "B" Coy on the front line with "D" Coy in Support and "C" Coy 16th Lancashire Fusiliers on Reserve in the REDAN. 16th Lancs Fusrs. on our left and 2nd Kings own Yorkshire Light Infantry on our right	R.W.R.
	21st-22nd		Battalion were relieved by the 16th Northumberland Fusiliers on relief Battalion returned to Brigade Reserve and took over the defences of NIEUPORT and PRESQUILE	R.W.R.
	24th-25th		Battalion relieved the 16th Northumberland Fusiliers in the Right Sub-Sector of the LOMBARTZYDE sector "A" & "C" Coys (being composite Coys held one Coys frontage) and "D" Coy on the front line with "B" Coy in Support and "B" Coy 16th Lancs Fusrs. in Reserve. 16th Lanc Fusrs on our left and 3/6 Att Royal Scots (14th Brigade) on our right	R.W.R. R.W.R.

WAR DIARY
or
INTELLIGENCE SUMMARY.
(Erase heading not required.)

Army Form C. 2118.

Place	Date	Hour	Summary of Events and Information	Remarks and references to Appendices
	Sept 29th		Battalion relieved by the 2nd K.O.Y.L.I. The latter were unlucky their advance party losing 3 Officers namely 1 killed and 2 wounded before the Regiment entered the line. On relief the Battalion marched to LA-PANNE and encamped. Casualties during tour Officers Wounded 1 Lieut. J. Acheson. Ranks killed 16 including 2649 L/Sjt E.J.Mr J. Amos who was supervising a working party outside Battn Headquarters whilst acting Regimental Sgt Major. Ranks wounded 45, of O.R's wounded 16. The sector that the Brigade was holding was most important as it was the main defence of the Bridges and Locks round NIEUPORT. In the event of these being lost the enemy would have been enabled to flood the country for a considerable distance; it was also important as the ground first in the rear of the front line was the only portion that could have been used as a jumping off place in the event of further operations. Previous to going into the line for above period there was reason to believe that the enemy attack was imminent. According to information received from a German prisoner the enemy had trenches laid out similar to the LOMBARTZYDE sector and were practising over same for an attack at an early date. In consequence of this special attention was paid to the wiring of this sector. Enemy artillery were exceptionally active throughout the period. Battn Headquarters and the 3rd and 4th lines being constantly shelled. Communication was interrupted daily. The CINQ PONTS. VAUXHALL. CROWDER and PUTNEY. BRIDGES over the YSER Canal being cut daily by the enemy shell fire.	
	Sept 30th		Battalion in LA-PANNE	

96/324.

2 R Lancs

Army Form C. 2118.

WAR DIARY
or
INTELLIGENCE SUMMARY.
(Erase heading not required.)

Instructions regarding War Diaries and Intelligence Summaries are contained in F. S. Regs., Part II. and the Staff Manual respectively. Title pages will be prepared in manuscript.

Place	Date	Hour	Summary of Events and Information	Remarks and references to Appendices
LA PANNE COXYDE	October 1917 1st and 2-4th		Battalion in billets in LA PANNE. Battalion marched to CANADA Camp COXYDE and billeted. Working parties were found by Battalion on front line system	S/A R S/A R
BRAY DUNES	5th		Battalion moved to BRAY DUNES to route march and billeted in B Camp	
BRAY DUNES	6th to 22nd		Remained in billets in BRAY-DUNES. Tactical Exercises. Field Days and Training carried out. Battalion also took part in two Brigade attack practices. The Officers Rugby team played two matches against Loos School losing the first by 9 pts to 5 pts and drawing the second by a good margin. In addition the Regt Football team played the 16th of Lancashire Fusrs and won by 3 goals to 1 goal. On Inter Coy League Competition was held and won by 'C' Coy. Officers and Sergeants played one match which was won by the Sergeants. (Capt. R. M. Vaughan joined Battn on 15th inst for duty)	S/A R S/A R S/A R
LA CASINO TETEGHAM	23rd 24th		Battalion moved by route march to LA-CASINO. TETEGHAM AREA and billeted in barns	
ERINGHAM	26th to 31st		Battalion marched to ERINGHAM AREA and billeted in barns Remained in billets in ERINGHAM AREA and were engaged in training and Field Days (Capt E. F. EAGER and 2/Lieuts Rees joined Battn and took over duties. G. O. C. 33nd Division delivered an address to 96th July Bde and complimented them on their very smart turn out and on their good work in the past of the line held by them during the last 4 months, also the fact the Battalion Football team played the 15th Lancashire Fusrs in the final round of the Bde competition and won by 2 goals to nil.	S/A R S/A R S/A R S/A R
	31st		On the night of the 27th Enemy aircraft returning from France in the neighbourhood dropped two bombs in the vicinity of Lt Capt billets, Casualties nil	S/A R S/A R

Army Form C. 2118.

WAR DIARY
or
INTELLIGENCE SUMMARY.
(Erase heading not required.)

V 51 4 0

Place	Date 1917	Hour	Summary of Events and Information	Remarks and references to Appendices
	Nov 1-11		Battalion remained in billets in ERINGHAM area, and engaged in Company, Battalion and Brigade Training. (teams were not sent home unless otherwise shown)	
	" 7-8		Headquarters Platoon won the Battalion Competition for the best Platoon in drill and handling of arms - thus qualifying to represent the Battalion in the Brigade Competition	
	" 8		First round Bde football Competition - beat the 16th Lanc. Fusiliers - 1 goal to nil	
	" 9		Combined Rugby football team of 16th Northumberland Fus. and 2nd Royal Innuskilling Fus. were beaten by 15th Lancs Fus. - score 12 pts - 3 pts. Battalion marched to ARKEKE and billeted there for the night	
	" 10		Second round Brigade football Competition - beat 16th Northumberland Fus. 2 goals - nil - thus qualifying to represent the Bde in the Divisional Competition	
	" 12		Battalion marched to WINNEZELLE Area and encamped there for the night.	

Army Form C. 2118.

WAR DIARY
or
INTELLIGENCE SUMMARY.
(Erase heading not required.)

Place	Date	Hour	Summary of Events and Information	Remarks and references to Appendices
	1917 Nov	13	Battalion marched to SCHOOL CAMP (L.3.a) and billeted	JMcK
	"	13-23	Battalion remained in billets in SCHOOL CAMP and was engaged in Company training and also furnished working parties for cleaning up Camp &c	JMcK
	"	17	Won the Brigade Cross Country Run, totalling 350 points – runners up 720 points – securing the following places, viz:- 1 – 3 – 5 – 10 – 14 – 19 – 21 – 22 – 23 – 25 – 26 – 28 – 30 – 31 – 39 – 41 – 48 – 56 – 60 – 68, out of a field of about 140 starters	JMcK
	"	20	Final of the Divisional football Competition beaten by 17th H.L.I., 2 goals – nil – An exceedingly good match on both sides – up to within 15 minutes of full time there had been no score by either side.	JMcK
	"	23	Battalion marched to BRAKE CAMP and billeted	JMcK

WAR DIARY
or
INTELLIGENCE SUMMARY.
(Erase heading not required.)

Army Form C. 2118.

Place	Date	Hour	Summary of Events and Information	Remarks and references to Appendices
	1917 Nov. 23-26		Battalion remained billeted in BRAKE CAMP and was engaged in Company Training and general cleaning up of Camp.	JMR
	" 26		Battalion marched to DIRTY BUCKET CAMP and entrained for IRISH FARM. Detrained at IRISH FARM and moved to WURST FARM by route march and relieved the 2nd Kings Own Yorkshire Light Infantry, 97th Infantry Brigade in Brigade Reserve.	JMR
	" 27		Battalion marched to trenches - SPRIET Sector - and relieved 16th H.L.I. - 15th Bonns Fuslrs on our left. 2nd Cectish Rifles, 25th Bde, 8th Division on our right, on night of 27th inst - 2nd Devons - 25th Bde, 8th Division on our right from 28 - 30th inst. 1st Royal Irish Rifles 23rd Bde, 8th Division on our right on night of 30th inst.	JMR

WAR DIARY
or
INTELLIGENCE SUMMARY.
(Erase heading not required.)

Army Form C. 2118.

Place	Date	Hour	Summary of Events and Information	Remarks and references to Appendices
	1917 Nov 30		Battalion relieved in trenches in SPRIET Sector by 16th North'umberland Fuslrs and withdrew to IRISH FARM and encamped Casualties during tour - 2nd Lieut J. Ryder wounded - Capt. C. Rundall M.C. killed, 2nd Lt J. Nagle 5" R.D.F. (attached) wounded - Other Ranks, killed 17, wounded 72, missing 29 The line which consisted of shell-holes or small portions of trenches ran from TEALL COTTAGES (V.30.c.1.5) to (V.29.b.0.6). The Companies held about 250 yds each, from right to left, "A" "B" "C" "D". Battalion H'qtrs was in a full-lict at MEETCHEELE. There was no cover for any movement between Bn H'qtrs and front line during the day. On the 30th, under cover of a very heavy barrage the enemy succeeded in capturing TEALL COTTAGES	PMR

WAR DIARY
or
INTELLIGENCE SUMMARY.
(Erase heading not required.)

Army Form C. 2118.

Place	Date	Hour	Summary of Events and Information	Remarks and references to Appendices
	1917 Nov 30		After dark on the same day Capt. Cundall M.C. was visiting his line and on going up to the post at YEALL COTTAGES, was fired at from very short range, and killed instantly.— He also lost 14 Other Ranks when the post was taken.	[initials]
			Under arrangements of 2nd Lieut Martin and several N.C.O' men, a Concert was given to all ranks of the Battalion in the Recreation hut, SCHOOL CAMP on the 20th inst. The G.O.C. 96th Infantry Bde was present and congratulated the Battalion on the success of the concert.	[initials]

[signatures]
EM Legg a/Lt
Cmg 2 Royal Inniskilling Fusiliers

Confidential   2nd Battn. Royal Inniskilling Fusiliers

Army Form C. 2118.

WAR DIARY
INTELLIGENCE SUMMARY

(Erase heading not required.)

VOLUME XLI   From 1st December 1917 to 31st December 1917

Place	Date 1917	Hour	Summary of Events and Information	Remarks and references to Appendices
CANAL BANK	Dec 10th		Battalion moved to billets at CANAL BANK. Remained in billets at CANAL BANK	Ref Maps Belg. ST. JULIEN
WURST FARM (support Battn)	Dec 11th	6.9a	Battalion marched to the line and was accommodated in Bivouacs at WURST FARM	ZONNEBEKE WESTROOSEBEKE
	" 12th	10a	Battalion relieved the 12th London Regiment 175th Infantry Brigade. 5th Division in the line between approximate front Y.21.c.1.1 or rather the LEKKERBOTTERBEEK at approximate front Y.21.c.1.1. or rather disposition of coys were as follows. C Coy on right D Coy on Rt. A Coy in support in vicinity of BURNS HOUSE and B Coy in reserve at WINCHESTER FARM. Battalion Headquarters HUBNER FARM. Right Coy SOUND FARM. Left Coy SHAFT V.29.a.05.45. 2/5th London Regiment on left. 16th Lancashire Fusiliers on right.	ZONNEBEKE RUR
FRONT LINE		12h	Inter Coy relief took place A Coy relieving C Coy on the right and B Coy relieving D Coy on the left. 4/5th London Reg.t relieved the 2/5th London Reg.t on our left.	RUR
		13th	Battalion was relieved on the line by 16th Northumberland Fusrs and withdrew to WURST FARM where it was in Brigade support and employed on carrying parties to Battalions in front line	RUR
WURST FARM				
		14th	96th Infantry Brigade were relieved on the line by the 97th Infantry Brigade. The Battalion was relieved by the XI Border Regt and entrained at CORNER COT on light railway, detraining at TROIS TOURS and marched to DAMBRE CAMP	RUR
DAMBRE CAMP				

WAR DIARY or INTELLIGENCE SUMMARY

Army Form C. 2118.

Place	Date	Hour	Summary of Events and Information	Remarks and references to Appendices
	Dec 21st		Battalion entrained at TROIS TOURS on light railway detraining at BATTLE SIDING and marched to HILLTOP FARM where it was engaged on work on the front line and on salvage work	ST JULIEN 28 N.W.2 20.6.A
HILLTOP FARM	" 25th		Christmas Day. no account of the Division being in the line. Christmas Day was not observed. The season's greetings and a letter of congratulation from Major General C.D. Shute. C.B. C.M.G. (Commanding 32nd Division) was received and circulated to the Battalion	21 D.1.5 RMR
	" 26th		at about 8.30 pm on account of an S.O.S sent up by the Division on our right the Battn was ordered to stand to and hold themselves in readiness to meet an short notice. at 8.45 pm this was cancelled as there had been no enemy attack.	RMR
Jun Coys IRISH FARM	" 27th		A and D Coys moved to IRISH FARM and took over huts evacuated by 2nd Battn. K.O.Y.L.I.	ST JULIEN 27.a.2.6 RMR
	" 28th		Transport travelled by road to the new area and the 50 men who were employed loading baggage and stores under Lieut. R.F.LEMANE travelled by train from VLAMERTINGHE Station	RMR
HILLTOP FARM to BONNIGUES	" 29th		Battalion was relieved by 17th Battn Notts and Derby Regiment in HILLTOP FARM and marched less Transport and 50 men (25 of C Coy and 25 of D Coy) to ST JEAN Station. IRISH FARM and entrained for AUDRUICQ at 4.20 pm from which place it marched to BONNIGUES arriving there about 2 am on 30th inst.	RMR Rijnshap. HAZEBROUCK 6a

Army Form C. 2118.

WAR DIARY
or
INTELLIGENCE SUMMARY.
(Erase heading not required.)

Instructions regarding War Diaries and Intelligence Summaries are contained in F. S. Regs., Part II. and the Staff Manual respectively. Title pages will be prepared in manuscript.

Place	Date	Hour	Summary of Events and Information	Remarks and references to Appendices
BONNINGUES	Dec 30th		Transport and the remainder of the Battalion arrived in billets at BONNINGUES at 10 am	
	31st		Battalion spent a quiet day in billets and was employed in cleaning up and refitting. The preliminaries for an Inter Football competition were arranged for order to be able to commence playing as soon as thaw sets in. Casualties during tour in Trenches Officers. Wounded 1. 2/Lieut. J. F. LACY. 2nd Irish Regiment att Wnd Batn Rl Inniskilling Fus. Ranks. Killed 5. Wounded 26. missing 10	

R.W. Pigg Lieut Col
Cmg 2 Bn Rl Inniskilling Fusiliers.

Confidential

WAR DIARY of 2nd Batn Royal Inniskilling Fusiliers Army Form C. 2118.

INTELLIGENCE SUMMARY.
(Erase heading not required.)

From 1st January 1918 to 31st January 1918

Place	Date 1918	Hour	Summary of Events and Information	Remarks and references to Appendices
BONNINGUES	Jan 1st to 16th		Battalion in billets in BONNINGUES. Training was carried out as far as weather would permit.	8/2
	5th		Xmas was observed as Christmas Day, as on December 26th the Battalion was in close support and no festivities could be arranged.	8/2
	19th		96th Infantry Brigade moved by road and rail to HOSPITAL FARM area. Battalion moved less transport by rail, entraining at AUDRICQ and detraining at ELVERDINGHE from which place they marched to "O" section DIRTY BUCKET Camp.	8/2
DIRTY BUCKET CAMP	21st		Transport which had travelled from BONNINGUES by road rejoined Battalion. The Battalion was for the first-time since hostilities began billeted in close proximity to the 1st Battalion. It is interesting to note that the 1st Battalion was commanded by Lieut. Col. J. R. Crawford D.S.O. who commanded this Battalion from 4.2.16 to 4.5.17. The two Battalions met in a friendly football match which was won by the 2nd Battalion by 3 goals to nil. After the match the W.Os and Sergts of the 1st Batn were entertained by the W.Os and Sergts of the 2nd Battalion.	8/2
				Sheet 28 N 1
CANAL BANK	22nd		Battalion moved to CANAL BANK.	C. 19. c.
			Remained in billets at CANAL BANK. The whole Battalion was engaged in work on the Army Line and each day a proportionate number of Officers and N.C.Os reconnoitred the line prior to taking over.	8/2
	23rd		1 Officer and 60 O.Ranks were attached to the 173 Tunnelling Coy R.E. for work on the Corps Line.	P.R. P.R.

Army Form C. 2118.

WAR DIARY
or
INTELLIGENCE SUMMARY.
(Erase heading not required.)

Instructions regarding War Diaries and Intelligence Summaries are contained in F.S. Regs., Part II. and the Staff Manual respectively. Title pages will be prepared in manuscript.

Hour, Date, Place	Summary of Events and Information	Remarks and references to Appendices
LARRY CAMP January 25th 1918	Battalion moved to LARRY CAMP and took over from Bttlt. vacated by 8th Suffolk Regt.	M
25th to 28th	Remained in Billets in LARRY Camp	M B.9.d.
29th	Battalion entrained at ELVERDINGHE station and proceeded by light railway to RUGBY CROSS ROADS, where guides met them and conducted them to the line where they relieved the 18th Middlesex Regt. in the right sector of the right sub-sector of the Bixschoot front. 14th Lancashire Fusiliers 35th Division on our right and 16th Lancashire Fusiliers on our Left. Battalion Headquarters after the Headquarters of the 18th Middlesex Regt at PASCAL FARM but on completion of relief moved to EGYPT HOUSE. 'B' Coy Headquarters taking over PASCAL FARM. During our tour in the line the enemy activity was practically nil, but at times we were bothered by machine Gun fire. Battalion Headquarters at EGYPT HOUSE was under direct observation from	M 26 N.W. C1 a. M BIXSCHOOTE. V7 a 9.3 – M U 6 c 6.0. M U 12 c 5.1 M U 12 b 2.9. M

Forms/C. 2118/11

WAR DIARY
or
INTELLIGENCE SUMMARY.
(Erase heading not required.)

Army Form C. 2118.

Hour, Date, Place	Summary of Events and Information	Remarks and References to Appendices
Jan 29th	(continued) the enemy thus preventing movement of any kind during the day time.	
31st	The Battalion was relieved in the line by the 16th Northumberland Fusiliers and entrained at RUGBY CORNER for DROMORE CROSS ROADS from where it marched to HOSPITAL FARM and was accommodated in Huts. Casualties during tour 4 O'Ranks wounded	
HOSPITAL FARM		

Major
Commanding 2/Rl Inniskilling Fusiliers